stre

ABERDEEN

Contents

Key to street map symbols	2
Key to street map pages	3
City centre map	4-5
Street maps	6-41
Local information	42-43
Places of interest	44-47
Key to road map symbols	48
Key to road map pages	49
Road maps	50-55
Index to street names	56-69
Index to place names	70-72

Published by Collins
An imprint of HarperCollins*Publishers*
77-85 Fulham Palace Road, Hammersmith, London W6 8JB
www.collins.co.uk

Copyright © HarperCollins*Publishers* Ltd 2003
Collins® is a registered trademark of HarperCollins*Publishers* Limited
Mapping generated from Collins Bartholomew digital databases

This product uses map data licensed from Ordnance Survey ® with the permission of the Controller of Her Majesty's Stationery Office.
© Crown copyright. Licence number 399302
The grid on this map is the National Grid taken from the Ordnance Survey map with the permission of the Controller of Her Majesty's
Stationery Office.

Printed in Hong Kong   ISBN 0 00 715675 8   QI11472 UDM   Imp 001
e-mail: roadcheck@harpercollins.co.uk

HarperCollins*Publishers*

2 Key to street map symbols

A90	Primary road dual/single		Restricted access street
A944	A Road dual/single		Pedestrian street
B9077	B Road dual/single	— — — —	Minor road/Track
	Other road dual/single	— — — _FB_	Footpath/Footbridge
	Road under construction	– ■ – ■ – ■	Unitary authority boundary
Toll	One-way street/Toll		Postcode boundary

	Railway line	P+🚌	Park & Ride
	Level crossing/ Railway tunnel	P	Car Park
	Railway station	— — — — —	Vehicle Ferry
	Bus/Coach station	— — — — —	Pedestrian Ferry

	Leisure/Tourism		Education
	Multiplex cinema		Health
	Shopping/Retail		Industry/Commerce
	Administration/Law		Notable building

Pol	Police station		Major religious building
PO	Post Office	+ ☾ ☼	Church/Mosque/ Synagogue
		🎥	Cinema
Lib	Library		Theatre
■	Fire station/Ambulance station/Community centre	i i	Tourist information centre (all year/seasonal)

	Wood/Forest	▶	Golf course
	Park/Garden/Recreation ground	† † † †	Cemetery
	Public open space		Built up area

³15	National Grid reference	**15**▶	Page continuation numb

SCALE

0	1/4	1/2	3/4	1 mile

0	1/4	1/2	3/4	1	1¹/4	1¹/2 kilometres

1:15840   4 inches to 1 mile : 6.3 cm to 1 km

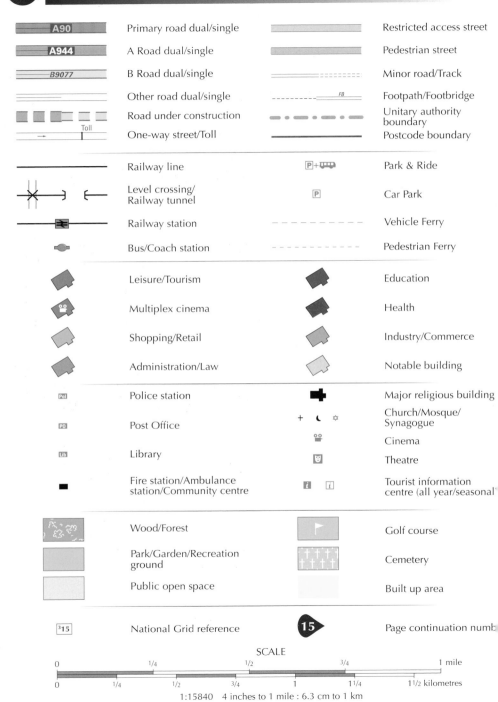

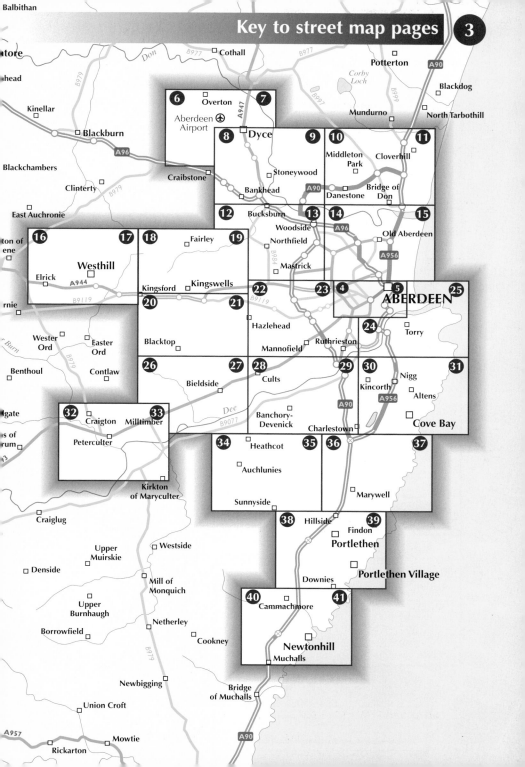

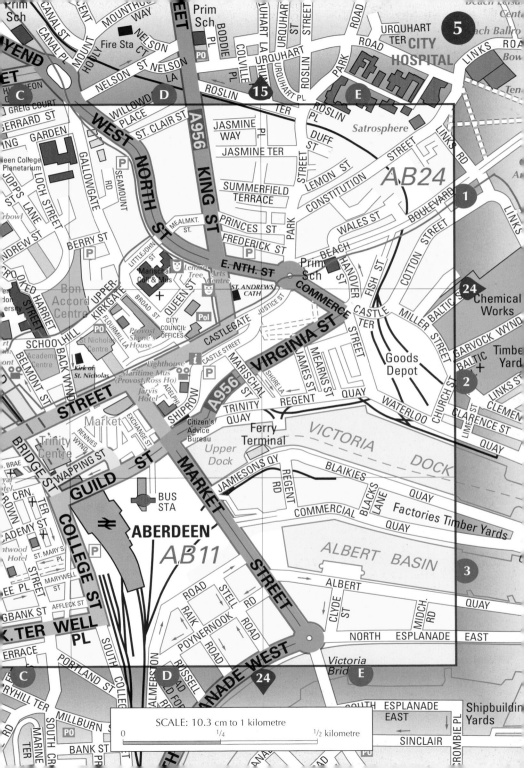

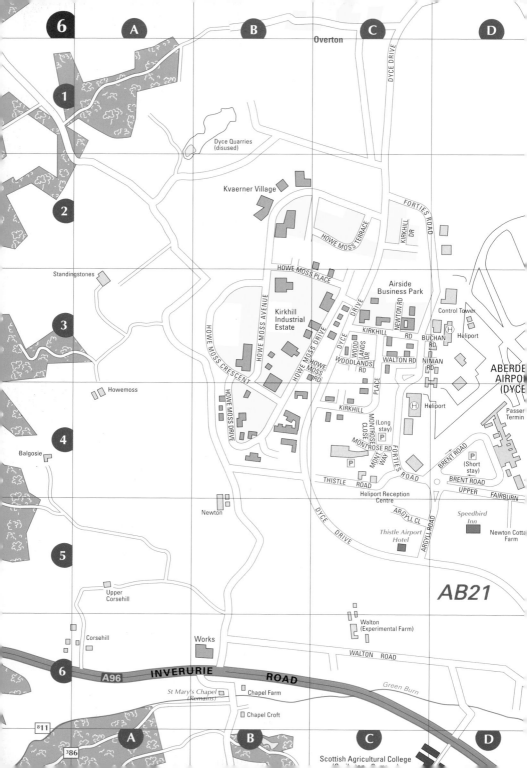

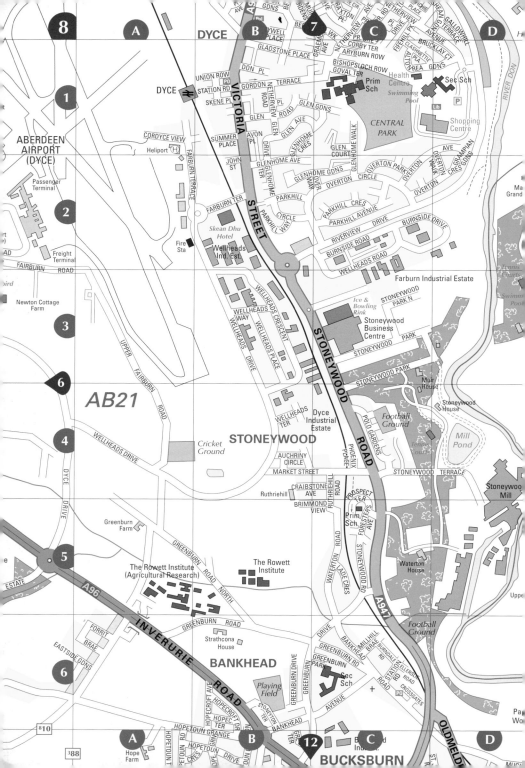

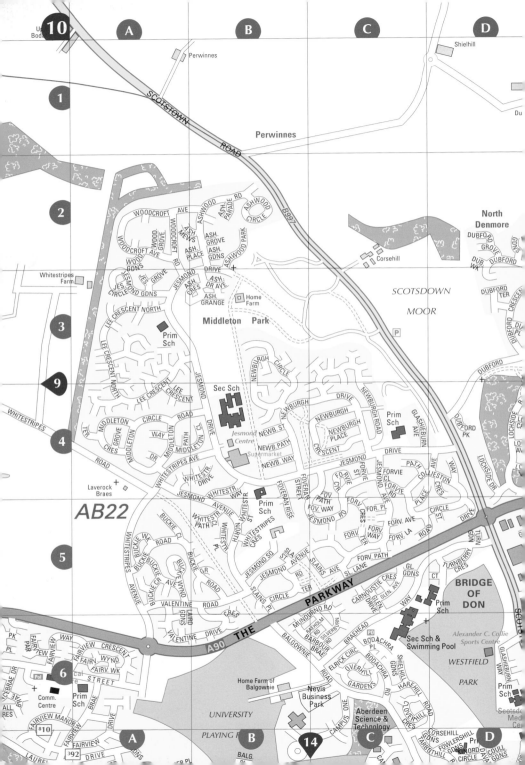

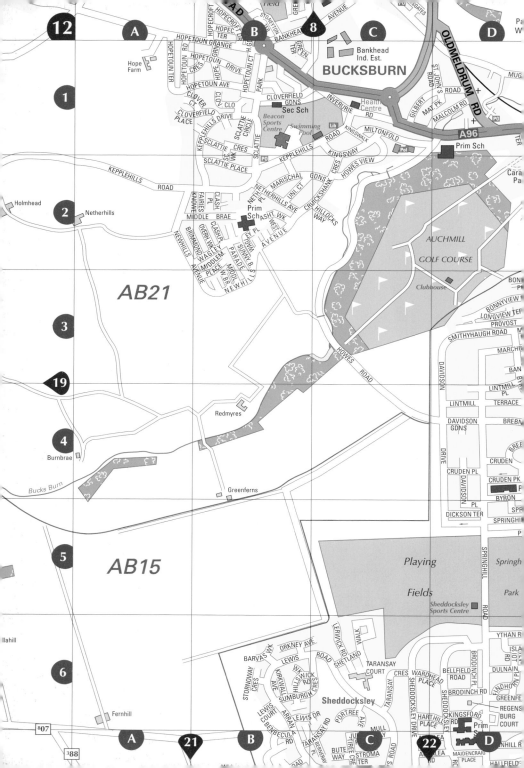

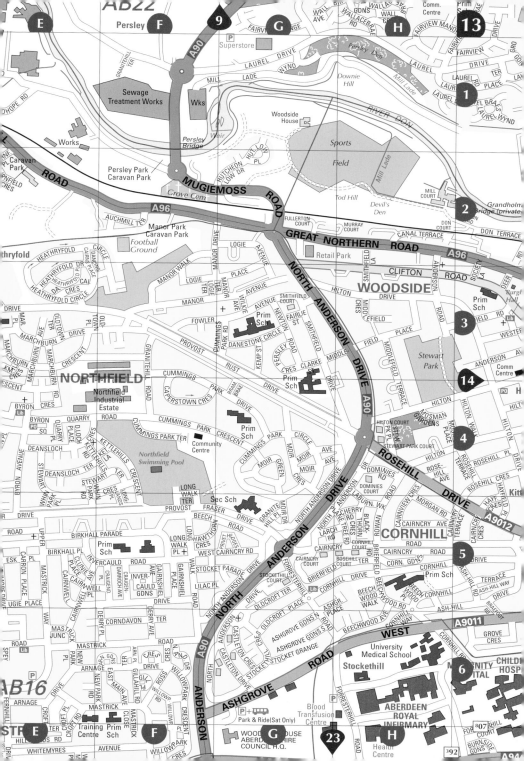

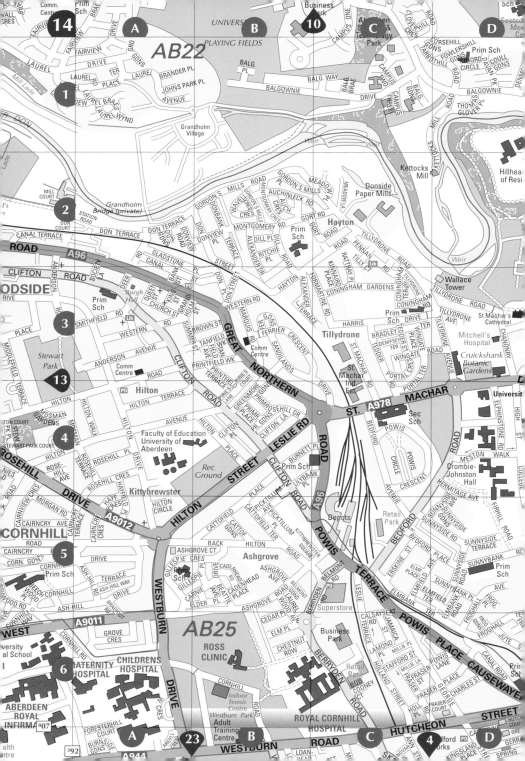

20

A   **B**   **18**   C   **D**

Cairnhillock

West Hatton

KINGSWOOD
AVE

KINGSWOOD
RD

B.D. PL   B.D. CL   B.D. AV

BROADDYKES AVE

BROAD VIEW

B.D. CRES

HUX
PL

HUX
CT

HUXTERSTONE DRIVE

HUXTERSTONE
TER

FAIRLEY
RD

FAIRLEY

EDMOND
GDNS

KINGSWOOD
GDNS

1

17

Kingsford

Home Farm

Park & Ride

2

A944   SKENE   ROAD

Braes of
Backhill

Backhill

3

KINGSHILL   WOOD

Upper
Kingshill

Craiglug

Upper
Fifeshill

King

4

Langside

Gairn

5

GAIRNHILL

WOOD

COUNTESSWELLS

FOREST

Blacktop

6

⁸04

³85

A   **B**   **26**   C   **D**

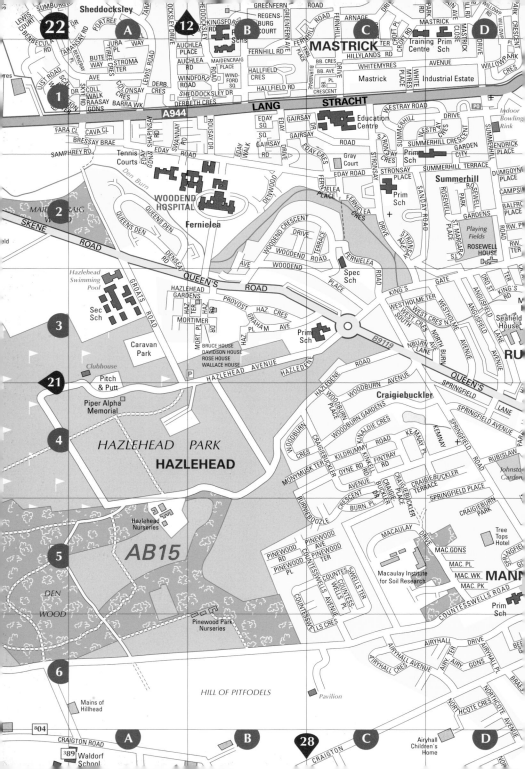

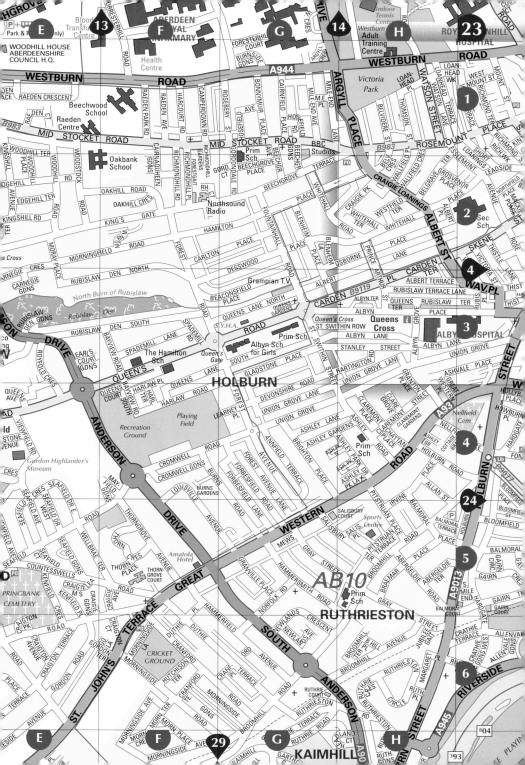

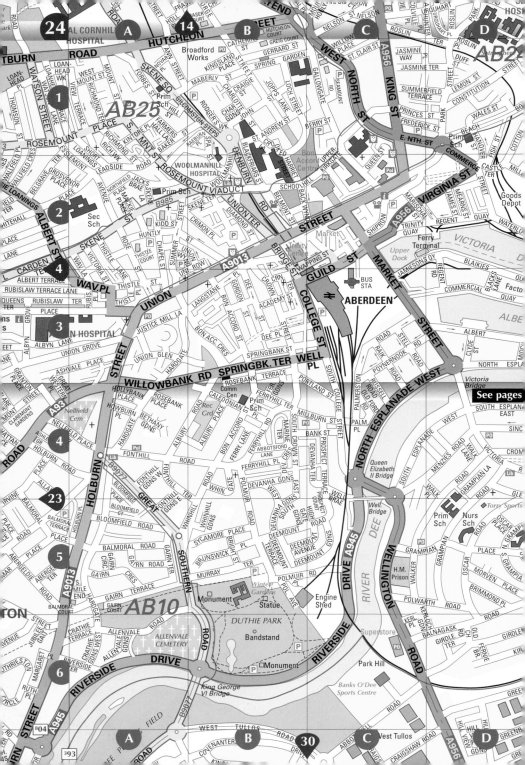

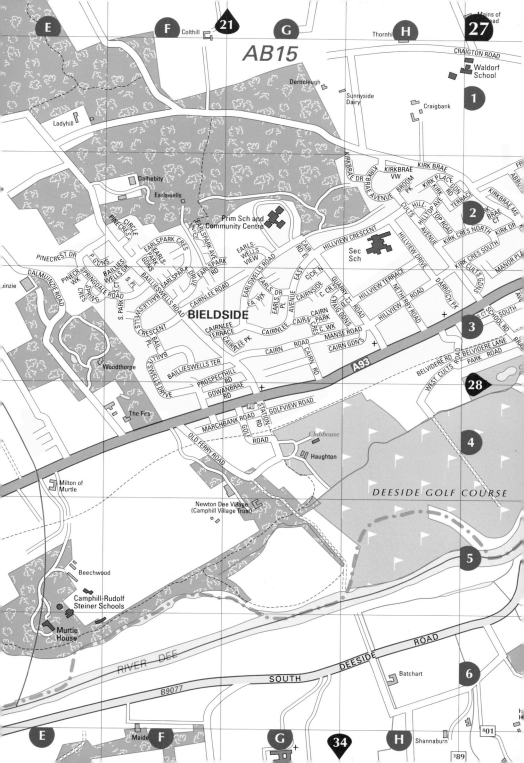

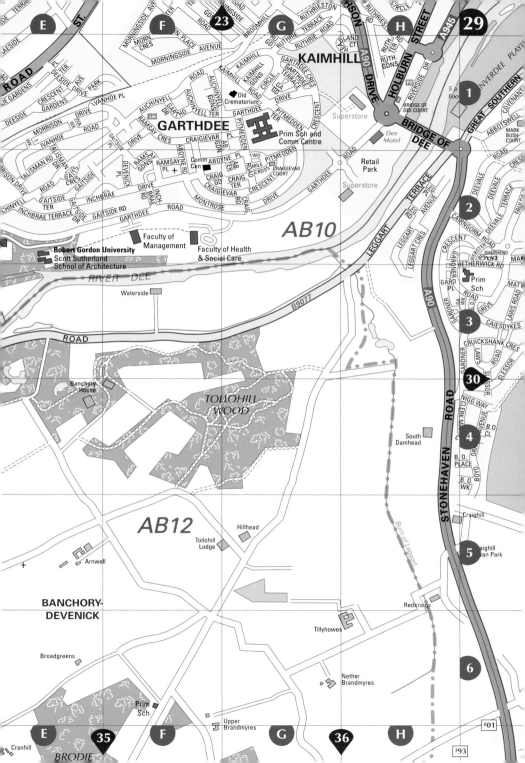

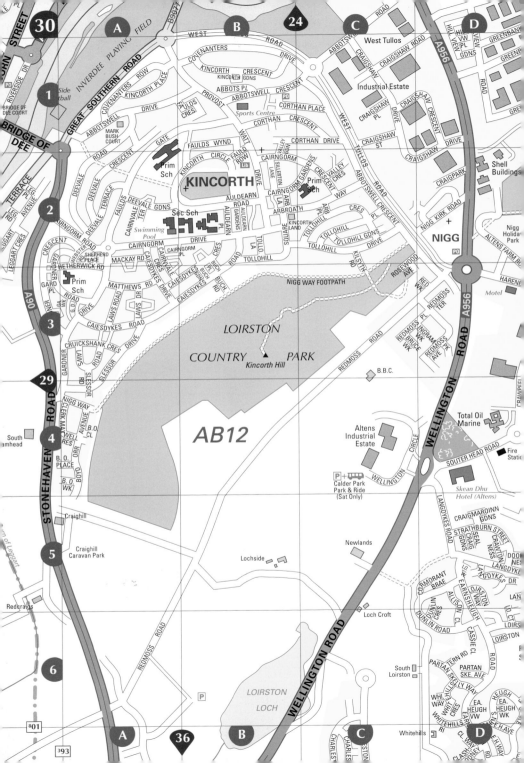

LOIRSTON COUNTRY PARK

Tullos Cairn

Needle's Eye

1

Baron's Cairn

Crab's Cairn

Doonies
Model
Farm

Doonies
Yawns

Peterseat

Adam's Pots

2

Peterseat
Park

North
Broad
Craig

Cat Cairn

PETERSEAT   DRIVE

Long Slough
Cave of Red Rocks

MINTO   AVENUE

MINTO   DRIVE

Robin Hood
Yawns

3

MINTO   AVENUE

MINTO   DRIVE

MINTO   ROAD

ALTENS
Aberdeen
College

Hasman
Rocks

Aberdeen   College   ROAD

HARENESS
PK

CIRCLE

Altens
Haven

HARENESS

MINTO   ROAD

Seals Hole

4

Altens
Industrial Estate

BLACKNESS   ROAD

BLACKNESS
AVE

Burnbanks Haven

OUTER   HEAD   ROAD

Burnbanks
Village

Souter Head

5

SUSAN   NESS
SKELLY
ROCK
FINDON   NESS

URDIE
CRESS

MON   NESS
ST
MARCHM   PL
SHIELDHILL   GDNS
MARCHM   GDNS

Bunstane Cove

ANNAT
BANK
TOD
GDNS

Well Cove
Black Cove

CATTO   CRES   LOIR   RD

MANOR

Cove
Rangers
F.C.

The Poor Man

6

CATTO   CRES

FALKLAND   AVE

LOIRSTON   ROAD

NBUTTS   CRES

The Graves

SIN   PL
SIN   TER

LOIRSTON   PL

**COVE
BAY**

WOOD   CRE

COLSEA   TER

COLS

Crawpeel Shore

A

27

B

C

28

D

Heathcot ...se

Jockston

Shannaburn

Mains of
Heathcot

Burn of Ardoe

1

The
Blairs
Museum

Westerton

Townhead

Marybrae

Kiln Burn

Shanna Burn

2

Hillhead of
Heathcot

Rowacks

3

CRAIGINGLES

WOOD

Auchlunies

Cowford

4

Prim
Sch

Newlands

5

Sunnyside

Bishopsto...

CLOCHANDIGHTER

6

...of
Patenlaws

Redmyre

Sunnyside

E
F
G
29
Prim
Sch
H
35
Brandmyres

Cranhill

BRODIE
WOOD

1

Townhead
Cottages

CRAN HILL

Woodside Farm

2

Drumth
Whacket

Jameston

3

Scatterburn

36

AB12

4

Haremoss

DUFF'S

HILL

5

Heathfield

Causeyport

6

Schoolhill

E
F
38
G
H
798
Moss-sid
392

WHI WAY
WHIT CRES
EA. HEUGH CL.
EA. HEUGH
FITTICK PLACE
PINE WOOD PL
SIN. PL
SIN. TER
ROAD
BURNBRAES PL
The Graves

Whitehills
WHITEHILLS RI
EARNSHEUGH
CL. WAY
E.A.H.WAY
E.H.WAY
E. H. CRES
MAR
REDWOOD CRES
COLSEA
PL
COLSEA RD
Crawpeel Shore

Prim Sch
CLASH
RODNEY
RO.
CL.
WK
CL. AVE.
COVE ROAD
PO
COVE ROAD
SPARK TER
COLSEA TER
STONEYHILL TER
COLSEA ROAD
Long Craig

CHARLESTON WAY
CHARLESTON ROAD
SNOS
SCYLLA DRIVE
COVE WYND
COVE WK
COVE CIRCLE
COVE CIRCLE
COVE GDNS
PATH
SEAVIEW TER
1

CHARLESTOWN WK
CHARL CIRCLE
COVE ROAD
CREEL DR
CREEL GDN
COVE WK
COVE CRESCENT
COVE GDNS
COVE PL
Harbour Cove Shore

CREEL ROAD
CREEL CT
CREEL AVE
CREEL PLACE
COVE
The Priest

CHARLESTOWN
CREEL WYND
The Kettle
2

Rigifa Farm

South Blackhill
Hare Ness
3

Blackhills of Cairnrobin
Horse Shoe

Bareside Point
4

Blowup Nose
5

Red Mantle
6

Earnsheugh Bay

Clashfarquhar

Bay

Berrymuir Head

1

Burn of Daff

Clashfarquhar Bay

2

Cobleboards

Cran
Hill

Floors Craig

3

DUNLIN
COURT
PLOVER
COURT
FULMAR
COURT
TURNSTONE
COURT
TERN
COURT
FFIN
URT
SANDERLING
COURT

Craig Stirling

RD
CRANHILL PL
CRAIG
MURRAY RD
AN.
RAE
T'RIDGE RD
ERAW RD
PO
RD
CHAPEL
RD
HEAD
AND.
DR
VILLA RD
SOUTH HEADLANDS CRES

*Newtonhill
Bay*

Whiteland Head

4

*ling
een*

5

May
Craig

6

USEFUL INFORMATION

Aberdeen and Grampian Tourist Board, 27 Albyn Place AB10 1YL
Tel: 01224 288828   www.agtb.org   **4 A3**

Central Library, Rosemount Viaduct AB25 1GW
Tel: 01224 652500   **4 C2**

Grampian Police, Force Headquarters, Queen Street
AB10 1ZA   *Tel: 01224 386000*
www.grampian.police.uk   **5 D2**

ADMINISTRATION

Aberdeen City Council *www.aberdeencity.gov.uk*
St. Nicholas House, Broad Street AB10 1BX
Tel: 01224 522000   **5 D2**

Town House, Broad Street AB10 1AQ
Tel: 01224 522500   **5 D2**

38 Powis Terrace, Kittybrewster AB25 3RF
Tel: 01224 480281   **14 C5**

ENTERTAINMENT
Cinemas
The Belmont, 49 Belmont Street AB10 1JS
Tel: 01224 343536/343534
www.picturehouse-cinemas.co.uk   **5 C2**

Lighthouse Cinema, 10 Shiprow AB11 5BY
Tel: 0870 240 4442   **5 D2**

UGC Cinemas, Queens Links Leisure Park, Leisure Road
AB11 5BT   *Tel: 01224 572228   0870 1550502*   **25 E1**

FURTHER EDUCATION

Aberdeen College, Gallowgate Centre, Gallowgate
AB25 1BN   *Tel: 01224 612000*
www.abcol.ac.uk   **5 C1**

HEALTH
Grampian University Hospitals NHS Trust
www.show.scot.nhs.uk/guh
Aberdeen Royal Infirmary, Foresterhill AB25 2ZN
Tel: 01224 681818   **13 H6**

Aberdeen Maternity Hospital, Foresterhill, Cornhill Road
AB25 2Z   *Tel : 01224 840606*   **14 A6**

Raeden Centre, Midstocket Road AB15 5PD
Tel: 01224 321381   **23 E1**

Royal Aberdeen Children's Hospital, Foresterhill,
Cornhill Road AB25 2ZG   *Tel: 01224 681818*   **14 A6**

Roxburghe House, Tor-Na-Dee Hospital,
Milltimber AB13 0HR   *Tel: 01224 681818*   **26 C4**

Tor-Na-Dee Hospital, Milltimber AB13 0HR
Tel: 01224 681818   **26 C4**

HELP AND ADVICE
Childline *Tel: 0800 1111   www.childline.org.uk*

Citizen's Advice Bureau, 47 Market Street AB11 5PZ
Tel: 01224 586255   www.nacab.org.uk   **5 D2**

Missing Persons *Tel: 0500 700 700*
www.missingpersons.org
NSPCC Helpline *Tel: 0808 8005000*
www.nspcc.org.uk

MEDIA
Local Newpapers
Aberdeen & District Independent   *Tel: 01224 618300*
www.aberdeen-indy.co.uk

Main Post Offices
St.Nicholas Shopping Centre, St. Nicholas Street
AB10 1HW   *Tel: 01224 633065* **5 D2**

489 Union Street AB11 6AZ   *Tel: 01224 581041*
www.royalmail.com   **4 B3**

Visitor Information Centre, 23 Union Street
AB11 5BP   *Tel: 01224 288828*   **5 D2**

74-76 Spring Garden AB25 1GN
Tel: 01224 522020   **5 C1**

Summerhill Education Centre, Stronsay Drive
AB15 6JA   *Tel: 01224 346060*   **22 C1**

Aberdeenshire Council *www.aberdeenshire.gov.uk*
Woodhill House, Westburn Road
AB16 5GB   *Tel: 01224 682222 / 0845 6067000*   **23 E1**

Theatres / Concert Halls
Arts Centre, 33 King Street AB24 5AA
Tel: 01224 635208   www.digifresh.co.uk   **5 D1**

Exhibition & Conference Centre, Bridge of Don AB23 8BL
Tel: 01224 824824   www.aecc.co.uk   **11 F5**

His Majesty's Theatre, Rosemount Viaduct AB25 1GL
Tel: 01224 641122   **4 C2**

Lemon Tree, Cafe Theatre, 5 West North Street AB24 5AT
Tel: 01224 642230   www.lemontree.org   **5 D1**

Music Hall, Union Street AB10 1QS
Tel: 01224 641122   **4 C2**

Robert Gordon University, Schoolhill AB10 1FR
Tel: 01224 262000   www.rgu.ac.uk   **5 C2**

University of Aberdeen, King's College AB24 3FX
Tel: 01224 272000   www.abdn.ac.uk   **14 D4**

Woodend Hospital, Eday Road AB15 6XS
Tel: 01224 663131   **22 B2**

Woolmanhill Hospital, Old Infirmary Buildings,
Woolmanhill AB25 1LD   *Tel: 01224 681818*   **4 C2**

Grampian Primary Care NHS Trust
Tel: 01224 663131   www.gpct.org.uk
Royal Cornhill Hospital, Cornhill Road AB25 2ZH   **13 H6**
City Hospital, Urquhart Road AB24 5AU   **15 F6**
Woodlands Hospital, Craigton Road, Cults AB15 9PR   **28 B1**

Independent Hospitals
Albyn Hospital, 21-24 Albyn Place AB9 1RJ
Tel: 01224 595993   www.ppphealthcare.co.uk   **4 A3**

Rape Crisis Centre *Tel: 01224 620772*
www.rapecrisis.co.uk/scottishnetwork.htm

RSPCA *Tel: 0870 444 3127   www.rspca.org.uk*
Samaritans, 60 Dee Street AB11 6DS
Tel: 01224 574488   Helpline: 08457 90 90 90
www.samaritans.org.uk

Victim Support Scotland
Tel: 01224 622478   Helpline: 0845 6039213
www.victimsupportsco.demon.co.uk

Aberdeen Press & Journal   *Tel: 01224 690222*
Aberdeen Evening Express   *Tel: 01224 690222*
Aberdeen Herald & Post   *Tel: 01224 690222*
www.thisisnorthscotland.co.uk

Local Radio
BBC Radio Scotland FM 92-95MHz, AM 810kHz
BBC Radio Nan Gaidheal AM990kHz
Tel: 08700 100 222   www.bbc.co.uk/scotland

Northsound One FM 96.9, 97.6, 103 MHz
Tel: 01224 337000   www.northsound1.co.uk

Northsound Two AM 1035 kHz
Tel: 01224 337000   www.northsound2.co.uk

43

SPORT & LEISURE

Golf

Auchmill Golf Club, Bonnyview Road,
West Heathryfold AB16 7FQ   Tel: 01224 714577   **12 D3**

Balnagask (Nigg Bay) Golf Club, St. Fitticks Road
AB11 9QT   Tel: 01224 876407   **25 G4**

Bon Accord Golf Club (Kings Links) Golf Road AB24 5QB
Tel: 01224 633464   **15 F5**

Caledonian Golf Club (Kings Links) Golf Road AB24 5QB
Tel: 01224 632443   **15 F5**

Deeside Golf Club, Golf Road, Bieldside
AB15 9DL   Tel: 01224 869457   **27 G4**

Hazlehead Golf Club, Hazlehead
AB15 8BD   Tel: 01224 321830   **22 A3**

Kings Links Golf Club, Golf Road AB24 1RZ
Tel: 01224 632269   www.kings-links.com   **15 F5**

Murcar Golf Club, Bridge of Don AB23 8BD
Tel: 01224 704354   www.murcar.co.uk   **11 H2**

Northern Golf Club (Kings Links) Golf Road AB24 5QB
Tel: 01224 636440   **15 F5**

Peterculter Golf Club, Oldtown, Burnside Road, Peterculter
AB14 0LN   Tel: 01224 735245
www.petercultergolfclub.co.uk   **32 D5**

Portlethen Golf Club, Badentoy Road,
Portlethen AB12 4YA   Tel: 01224 781090   **38 C2**

Royal Aberdeen Golf Club, Links Road,
Bridge of Don AB23 8AT   Tel: 01224 702571
www.royalaberdeengolf.com   **15 G1**

Westhill Golf Club, Westhill Heights, Westhill
AB32 6RY   Tel: 01224 742567   **16 C3**

Shopping

Aberdeen Market, 8-10, Market Street AB11 5NX
Tel: 01224 575576   **5 D2**

Academy Shopping Centre, Schoolhill AB10 1LB
Tel: 01224 633009
www.academyshoppingcentre.co.uk   **5 C2**

Bon Accord Centre, George Street AB25 1HZ
Tel: 01224 647470   **5 C2**

St. Nicholas Centre, St. Nicholas Street AB10 1HW
Tel: 01224 645420   www.st-nicholas.co.uk   **5 D2**

Trinity Shopping Centre, Union Street AB11 6BE
Tel: 01224 580076   **5 C2**

Sports Centres/Swimming Pools

Alexander C Collie Sports Centre, Cardens Knowe,
Scotsdown Road AB22 8PE   Tel: 01224 826769   **10 D6**

Banks O'Dee Sports Centre, Abbotswell Road
AB12 3AB   Tel: 01224 893333   **24 C6**

Beach Leisure Centre, Sea Beach, Esplanade
AB24 5NR   Tel: 01224 655401   **15 G6**

Beacon Sports Centre, Kepplehills Road
AB21 9DG   Tel: 01224 712889   **12 B1**

Bon Accord Baths & Leisure Centre, Justice Mill Lane
AB11 6EQ   Tel: 01224 587920   **4 B3**

Bucksburn Swimming Pool, Kepplehills Road
AB21 9DG   Tel: 01224 716479   **12 C1**

Hazlehead Swimming Pool, Groats Road
AB15 8BE   Tel: 01224 310062   **22 A3**

Jesmond Centre, Jesmond Drive AB22 8UR
Tel 01224 707090   **10 B4**

Kincorth Sports Centre, Corthan Crescent
AB12 5BB   Tel: 01224 879759   **30 B1**

Kincorth Swimming Pool, Cairngorm Drive
AB12 5NL   Tel: 01224 872227   **30 B2**

Lynx Ice Arena, Sea Beach, Esplanade
AB24 5NR   Tel: 01224 649930   **15 G6**

Northfield Swimming Pool, Kettlehills Crescent
AB16 5LR   Tel: 01224 680307   **13 F4**

Peterculter Sports Centre, Coronation Road, Peterculter
AB14 0RX   Tel: 01224 732069   **33 E3**

Sheddocksley Sports Centre, Springhill Road
AB16 6NZ   Tel: 01224 692534   **12 D5**

Torry Sports Centre, Oscar Road, Victoria Road
AB11 8ER   Tel: 01224 871213   **24 D5**

Tullos Swimming Pool, Girdleness Road AB11 8TD
Tel: 01224 878559   **25 E5**

Westburn Sports Centre, Westburn Park,
Westburn Road AB25 3DE   Tel: 01224 641719   **14 B6**

Westdyke Leisure Centre, 4 Westdyke Avenue, Elrick, Westhill
AB32 6QX   Tel: 01224 743098   **16 C5**

Westhill Swimming Pool, Hays Way, Westhill AB32 6XZ
Tel: 01224 744933   **17 E4**

Stadia

Aberdeen Football Club, Pittodrie Stadium, Pittodrie Street
AB24 5QH   Tel: 01224 632328   www.afc.co.uk   **15 F5**

Chris Anderson Stadium, Linksfield Road AB24 5RU
Tel: 01224 487371   **15 E4**

TRANSPORT

Air

Aberdeen Airport, Dyce AB21 7DU   Tel: 01224 722331
www.baa.co.uk/main/airports/aberdeen   **6 D4**

Ferry (to Orkney & Shetland)

North Link Ferries, Stromness, Orkney KW16 3BH
Tel: 01856 851 155   www.northlinkferries.co.uk   **5 D2**

Rail

Railway Station, Guild Street   **5 D3**
National Enquiries Tel: 08457 484950   www.networkrail.co.uk

Bus   Traveline: 0870 608 2608

Bus Station, Guild Street AB11 6GR   **5 D3**

First Aberdeen, 395 King Street AB9 1SP
Tel: 01224 650000   Information: 01224 650065
www.firstaberdeen.co.uk

Stagecoach Bluebird Buses, Guild Street AB11 6GR
Tel: 01224 212266   www.stagecoachbus.com/bluebird

Park & Ride Tel: 01224 650000:
   Exhibition and Conference Centre, Bridge of Don   **11 F6**
   Kingswells   **18 D6**
   Calder Park (Saturday only), Wellington Circle   **30 C4**
   Woodhill House (Saturday only), Westburn Road   **13 G6**

☐ Indicates a place of interest that appears in the street map pages. An explanation of the other symbols can be found on page 48.

☐ **Aberdeen Art Gallery**   5 C2
The gallery features Scottish, French and 20c English paintings and collections of silver and glass. Spencer, Nash, Bacon and sculptor Henry Moore are among British artists represented.

☐ **Aberdeen Maritime Museum**   5 D2
A museum focusing on fishing, shipbuilding and the off-shore oil industry with multi-media displays. Exhibits include a 22 foot (8.5 metre) high model of an oil platform and there is a collection of maritime paintings. The entrance to the 15c Provost Ross's house is through the museum.

🏛 **Aberdeenshire Farming Museum**   51 E3
A working farm and museum illustrating regional farming history, in Aden Country Park.

🅼 **Aberlemno Sculptured Stones**   54 D4
Located in the churchyard at Aberlemno, an upright cross slab (Historic Scotland) with Pictish symbols and combat relief. There are three other stones nearby, beside the B9134.

▨ **Aden Country Park**   51 E3
A country park covering 230 acres (93 hectares) on the Buchan estate, which dates from the 18c. Features include a wildlife discovery centre, sensory garden, ruined mansion, nature trails and woodland walks. It is also the location of the Aberdeenshire Farming Museum.

🏛 **Angus Folk Museum**   54 B5
Housed in a row of 18c cottages (National Trust for Scotland) in Glamis, the museum has a collection of 19c domestic furniture and memorabilia and also agricultural artefacts.

✠ **Arbroath Abbey**   55 E5
Substantial remains of a Tironensian monastery (Historic Scotland) in the centre of Arbroath. Founded in 1178 by William the Lion, King of Scots, the abbey is linked with Scottish nationalism. The Declaration of Arbroath asserting Scotland's independence from England was signed at the abbey in 1320, and the Stone of Destiny was found here in 1951, having been taken from Westminster Abbey. An abbot's house is among the most notable ruins.

🏛 **Arbuthnot Museum**   51 G3
Peterhead's local history museum with the emphasis on the fishing industry. The museum also includes an art gallery, large coin collection, Inuit artefacts and Arctic animals.

✠ **Arbuthnott Church**   55 G2
While the church is mainly 16c, the chancel dates from 1242.

▩ **Arbuthnott House**   55 F2
This 13c fortified home of the Arbuthnott family features a 17c walled garden.

▥ **Balbithan**   53 F2
A late 17c tower house surrounded by an attractive old-world garden.

▨ **Balmedie Country Park**   53 G2
Situated between Balmedie and Balmedie Beach, the country park has over 150 acres (60 hectares) of grassland, dunes and sandy beach. It attracts a wide variety of seabirds.

▥ **Barrie's House**   54 B4
This is the Kirriemuir birthplace of Sir J.M. Barrie, famous as the creator of Peter Pan. A former weaver's cottage (National Trust for Scotland), it is furnished as in Barrie's day. There is a Barrie exhibition in the adjacent house.

⚔ **Battle of Alford 1645**   52 C2
A battle site where Montrose defeated the Covenanters.

⚔ **Battle of Barra Hill 1308**   53 E1
Robert the Bruce decisively defeated John Comyn here on Christmas Eve.

⚔ **Battle of Corrichie 1562**   53 D3
The Earl of Huntly was defeated here by followers of Mary, Queen of Scots, led by the Earl of Moray.

⚔ **Battle of Harlaw 1411**   53 E1
It was here that Donald, Lord of the Isles, tried to claim the Earldom of Ross and was defeated by the Earl of Mar.

⚔ **Battle of Nechtanesmere 685**   54 D5
A battle on Dunnichen Hill where Egfrith of Northumbria was killed by the Picts, thereby ending Anglian incursions into the area.

⚔ **Battle of Turiff 1639**   50 C2
This is the site of the first skirmish in the Civil War, known as the 'Trot of Turriff', where the Royalist Gordons defeated the Covenanters.

🏰 **Boyne Castle**   50 B1
Ruins of the castle, located on the Burn of Boyne near Boyne Bay.

✠ **Brechin Cathedral**   55 D4
The cathedral was built in the 13c on the site of a previous foundation in the centre of Brechin. The Brechin Round Tower (Historic Scotland) is attached.

🅼 **Brechin Round Tower**   55 D4
An Irish-type round tower dating from the 11c (Historic Scotland) and attached to Brechin Cathedral in the centre of the city. It is one of only two such towers remaining on the Scottish mainland.

☐ **Bridge of Dee**   29 H1
Spanning the River Dee on the south approach to Aberdeen, the bridge has seven arches and dates from the 16c.

🅼 **Brown Caterthun**   55 D3
An Iron Age fort (Historic Scotland) with four concentric entrenchments.

▣ **Caen Lochan Nature Reserve**   54 A2
Situated in the mountains to the north west of Glendoll Lodge.

Caledonian Railway   55 E4
A tourist railway which runs 4m(6km) from the Victorian terminus at Brechin down a 1 in 70 gradient to Bridge of Dun, a junction of the former Strathmore main line.

Castle Fraser   53 E2
Built between 1575 and 1636, this baronial tower house (National Trust for Scotland) has a notable Great Hall and walled garden. It is said to be haunted.

Craig Castle   52 B1
Overlooking a wooded glen, the castle was built in the 16c and has the addition of an 18c portal and wing.

Craigievar Castle   52 C3
A 17c turreted baronial castle (National Trust for Scotland) with seven storeys and surrounded by notable grounds.

Craigston Castle   50 C2
Completed in 1607 and still owned by the original family. Interior decoration dates from the early 16c.

Crathes Castle   53 E4
Built in the 16c, the castle (National Trust for Scotland) also has later additions. The gardens include early 18c yew hedges and a walled garden.

Crombie Castle   50 A2
A medieval castle to the west of Aberchirder.

Crombie Country Park   54 D5
The 250 acre (100 hectare) park surrounds the Victorian Crombie Reservoir which was styled to resemble a natural loch.

Cruickshank Botanic Garden   14 D3
Owned by the University of Aberdeen, this 11acre (4 hectare) botanic garden in Aberdeen features a rock garden, herbaceous border and an arboretum.

Cullen House   50 A1
Lying to the south west of Cullen, the house is partly 13c.

Cullerlie Stone Circle   53 E3
(Also known as Garlogie Stone Circle.)
A Bronze Age stone circle (Historic Scotland) of eight boulders with a 30 foot (9 metre) diameter, enclosing excavated burial chambers.

Culsh Earth House   52 C3
A well preserved prehistoric earth house or souterrain (Historic Scotland) at Culsh.

Deer Abbey   51 E3
Scant remains of a 13c Cistercian monastery (Historic Scotland) which are situated on the north bank of South Ugie Water.

Delgatie (Delgaty) Castle   50 C2
An 11c inhabited tower house containing the widest turnpike stair in Scotland and painted ceilings.

Deskford Church   50 A1
The ruin of a small medieval church (Historic Scotland), containing a carved sacrament house, on the Burn of Deskford.

Doonies Farm   31 H1
Rare breeds working farm with Shetland ponies, Clydesdale horses, cattle, sheep and pigs.

Drum Castle   53 E3
A medieval square tower (National Trust for Scotland) with Jacobean and Victorian extensionsto the west of Peterculter. The grounds contain a unique Garden of Historic Roses, 16c chapel, and woodland walks.

Duff House   50 B1
Designed by William Adam for the first Earl of Fife in 1735, Duff House (Historic Scotland) at Banff is a fine example of Georgian baroque architecture. During World War II it housed prisoners of war but now contains collections of the National Galleries of Scotland.

Dunnottar Castle   53 F5
Dating in part from the late 14c, this ruined fortress of the Earls of Marischal is dramatically situated on a rock promontory and was used in Zeffirelli's film of Hamlet.

Duthie Park and Winter Gardens   24 B6
This 50 acre (20 hectares) park is renowned for the rose garden known as 'Rose Mountain' and the 2 acre Winter Gardens with a hothouse featuring exotic plants.

Dyce Symbol Stones   53 F2
Two Pictish symbol stones (Historic Scotland) which are to be found in the ruins of Dyce Old Kirk.

Eassie Sculptured Stone   54 B5
A good example of an elaborately carved early Christian monument (Historic Scotland) with a Celtic cross on one side and Pictish symbols on the reverse.

Easter (East) Aquhorthies   53 E1
The site of an ancient recumbent stone circle (Historic Scotland) to the west of Inverurie.

Eden Castle   50 B2
Ruins of a 16c tower house on the east side of River Deveron.

Ederdover Castle   55 E4
(See Red Castle)

Edzell Castle   55 D3
An early 16c tower house (Historic Scotland) with 17c alterations and additions by Sir David Lindsay. It includes Lindsay's formal decorated garden, or Pleasaunce. The castle was vandalised after the second Jacobite uprising.

Fasque House   55 E2
Once home of former Prime Minister William Gladstone, the interior of this 19c house is little changed since Gladstone's time. The house is surrounded by a deer park.

Finavon Castle   54 D4
Ruined 16c stronghold of the Earls of Crawford to the south of Finavon.

Finavon Doocot   54 D4
The largest dovecot (National Trust for Scotland) in Scotland with 2400 nesting boxes. Dates from the 16c.

Findlater Castle   50 A1
Once an Ogilvie stronghold, this ruined 15c castle is situated on cliffs to the east of Cullen.

Fyvie Castle   50 C4
Dating from the 14c with late 16c additions, the castle has been completely restored and is probably the grandest example of Scottish baronial architecture. Notable features include a wheel staircase, Victorian earth closet and a racquet court. Fyvie castle also has a collection of armour, paintings and 17c tapestries.

Fyvie Church   50 C4
The church is noted for its stained glass, 17c panelling and Celtic stones.

Glamis Castle   54 B5
Mainly 17c but with parts of much earlier, Glamis Castle is the family home of the Earls of Strathmore and Kinghorne and was the childhood home of HM Queen Elizabeth, the Queen Mother.

Glenbuchat Castle   52 A2
A ruined Z-plan stronghold of the Gordons dating from 1590 (Historic Scotland).

Glendronach Distillery   50 B3
Located in Glen Dronach, the distillery was built in 1926. It draws its water from Dronach Burn, which has previously made its way through rich peat beds.

Glengarioch Distillery   53 F1
One of Scotland's oldest distilleries, Glengarioch was founded in 1797 at Oldmeldrum. It is housed in a granite building at one end of the Garioch valley and draws its water from springs on Percock Hill.

Gordon Highlanders Museum   23 E4
Commemorating the regiment first raised by the Duke of Gordon in 1794, the museum displays uniforms, colours, weapons and paintings. It is housed in the former home of Victorian artist Sir George Reid in south west Aberdeen.

Grampian Transport Museum   52 C2
Historic vehicles of every description are displayed in this museum at Alford. Attractions include a driving simulator and a video bus presenting the history of road transport and motor sport.

Haddo House   51 D4
An elegant mansion of 1731 (National Trust for Scotland) designed by William Adam. Haddo House is the Seat of the Marquess of Aberdeen. It has a beautiful library and houses a permanent exhibition of James Giles' paintings. There is a terraced rose garden.

Haughton House Country Park   52 C2
Surrounding 19c Haughton House, the 48 acre (19 hectare) country park consists chiefly of woodland with gardens, an aviary and an adventure playground. The visitor centre has displays on local farming life and natural history.

Hazlehead Park   22 A4
Comprising woodland and rose gardens, this Aberdeen park also contains a pets corner, aquarium, walk-in aviary and maze.

House of Dun   55 E4
An 18c Palladian house (National Trust for Scotland) designed by William Adam and built for David Erskine, Lord Dun.

Huntly Castle   50 A3
The remains of a Gordon stronghold (Historic Scotland) beside the River Deveron to the north of Huntley. Partly 12c but mainly 16c, Huntly Castle has notable heraldic sculptures and inscribed stone friezes.

Kildrummy Castle   52 B2
A ruined 13c courtyard castle (Historic Scotland), a former stronghold of the Earls of Mar which was dismantled after the Jacobite rising of 1715. The gardens are notable for shrubs and alpines, and include water gardens and an ancient quarry.

King's College Visitor Centre   14 D4
A multi-media exhibition of Aberdeen University's 500 year history, housed in the Victorian King's Library Building, Old Aberdeen.

Kinkell Church   53 E2
The ruins of a 16c parish church with a fine sacrament house (Historic Scotland), to the south of Inverurie on the east side of the River Don. The grave slab of Gilbert of Greenlaw who was killed in battle in 1411 is to be found here.

Kinneff Church   55 G2
Part of the church formed the hiding place for the Scottish crown jewels smuggled from Dunnottar castle whilst under seige from Cromwell in 1651. The present church dates from 1738.

Leith Hall   52 C1
Home of the head of the Leith family since 1650, the 17c house (National Trust for Scotland) is built round a central courtyard. It contains a collection of military memorabilia and there are both formal and informal gardens.

Loanhead Stone Circle   53 E1
A Bronze Age stone circle (Historic Scotland) which encloses a ring cairn. There is also a small burial enclosure nearby.

Loch of Strathbeg   51 F2
Situated behind Strathbeg Bay, this land-locked coastal lagoon is 2miles (3km) long and has a RSPB reserve.

Loirston Country Park   30 B3
This 620 acre (250 hectare) country park to the south east of Aberdeen harbour has coastal walks and includes Girdle Ness lighthouse. It attracts a wide variety of seabirds and other wildlife.

Maiden Stone   53 E1
A 9c red granite Pictish symbol stone (Historic Scotland), with Pictish symbols carved on one side and a Celtic cross on the other. Maiden Stone is 10 feet (3 metres) high.

Marischal Museum   5 D1
Aberdeen University's anthropological museum in central Aberdeen with displays illustrating the archaeology and folk history of north east Scotland. Egyptian antiquities are amongst the other collections.

★ **Meffan Institute**　　　54 C4
Museum and art gallery at Forfar with Neolithic, Pictish and Celtic exhibits, and a section on 17c witch-hunting.

🏛 **Meigle Sculptured Stones**　　54 A5
Christian and Pictish inscribed stones (Historic Scotland) at Meigle. In the Meigle Museum, are housed approximately 30 other stones from the area, dating from 7c-10c.

🏛 **Memsie Cairn**　　　51 E1
Possibly dating from the Bronze Age, this is a fine example of a large stone cairn (Historic Scotland).

🏛 **Montrose Museum and Art Gallery**　55 F4
Montrose's local history museum with maritime and natural history exhibits and including the art gallery.

🏰 **Muchalls Castle**　　　53 F4
The 17c castle was destroyed by fire in the second Jacobite uprising and later rebuilt.

🏛 **Museum of Scottish Lighthouses**　51 E1
The museum is located at Kinnaird Head at Fraserburgh and commemorates Scottish lighthouses. Housed in the first lighthouse (Historic Scotland) built by the Northern Lighthouse Company in 1787, itself contained within a 16c castle built for the Fraser family, the museum includes the history of the Stevenson family, designers of many Scottish lighthouses.

🏛 **Peel Ring of Lumphanan**　　52 C3
A moated medieval motte (Historic Scotland) to the south west of Lumphanan, where it is said Macbeth made his last stand. The structure is 120 feet (36.5 metres) in diameter by 18 feet (5.5 metres) high.

★ **Peterhead Maritime Heritage**　51 G3
Centre
Illustrating the importance of maritime industries to Peterhead, the centre has displays on fishing, whaling and the oil industries.

🏛 **Picardy Stone**　　　50 B4
The stone dates back from the 7c or 8c and contains Pictish inscriptions (Historic Scotland).

🏰 **Pitcaple Castle**　　　53 E1
Lying to the north east of Pitcaple, a 16c Z-plan castle which was renovated in the 19c.

🌼 **Pitmedden Garden**　　　53 F1
National Trust for Scotland property which includes a 17c garden designed by Sir Alexander Seton, Baron of Pitmedden, and a Museum of Farming Life.

🏰 **Pitsligo Castle**　　　51 E1
Ruined castle of the Forbes family, dating from 1424, and now partly renovated.

❑ **Provost Ross's House**　　5 D2
15c home of a former Lord Provost of Aberdeen at Shiprow in Aberdeen. Entered from Aberdeen Maritime Museum, it now houses a National Trust for Scotland visitor centre.

❑ **Provost Skene's House**　　5 D2
A fine example of early burgh architecture in Guestrow, Aberdeen. Dating from the 16c, the house contains furnished period rooms, painted ceilings, a costume gallery and local history displays.

🏰 **Red Castle**　　　55 E4
(Also known as Ederdover Castle.)
Ruins of a 16c L-plan tower house on the south bank of the Lunan Water estuary to the north east of Inverkeilor.

✠ **Restenneth Priory**　　54 C4
The ruined chancel and tower of a 12c Augustinian priory church (Historic Scotland). The lower part of the tower is early Romanesque in style.

❑ **St. Machar's Cathedral**　　14 D3
A twin-towered 15c granite fortified cathedral built on an ancient site of worship in Aberdeen. The nave, dated 1520, is still used as a parish church. Features include a 16c oak heraldic ceiling and notable stained glass. The ruined transepts (Historic Scotland) contain the tomb of Bishop Dunbar.

✠ **St. Mary's Kirk**　　　52 B1
Roofless medieval parish church (Historic Scotland) at Auchindoir featuring a carved early Romanesque doorway and an early 14c sacrament house.

🏛 **St. Orland's Stone**　　54 C5
Symbol stone (Historic Scotland) depicting hunting and boating scenes.

❑ **Satrosphere**　　　5 E1
This hands-on science and technology discovery centre is situated in Aberdeen's old tramsheds and was the first of its kind in Scotland.

🏰 **Slains Castle**　　　51 G4
Site of a 19c castle, now demolished, on a granite headland above Port Errol.

❑ **Storybook Glen**　　　33 G5
Nursery and fairytale fantasyland and leisure park for children in landscaped gardens to the east of Kirkton of Maryculter.

❑ **The Blairs Museum**　　34 A1
Scottish Roman Catholic heritage collection of decorative art, church plate, and embroidered vestments with artefacts relating to the Stewarts and Mary Queen of Scots. The collection is housed in the former Roman Catholic school, Blairs College.

🏰 **Tolquhon Castle**　　　53 F1
The remains of a pink sandstone medieval castle (Historic Scotland) built for the Forbes family. Situated in a wooded glen to the north west of Pitmedden, the ruin includes a 15c-16c tower and an ornamented gatehouse.

🏛 **Tomnaverie Stone Circle**　　52 B3
Stones dating from 1800-1600 BC (Historic Scotland) on a rocky knoll to the south east of Tarland.

🏰 **Towie Barclay Castle**　　50 C3
Remains of a ruined 16c castle to the south of Mains of Towie.

🏛 **White Caterthun**　　　54 D3
Well-preserved Iron Age fort (Historic Scotland) with a massive stone rampart.

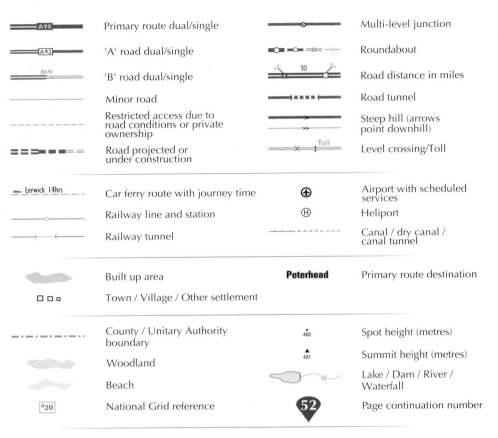

A90	Primary route dual/single	Multi-level junction	
A92	'A' road dual/single	Roundabout	
B979	'B' road dual/single	Road distance in miles	10
	Minor road	Road tunnel	
	Restricted access due to road conditions or private ownership	Steep hill (arrows point downhill)	
	Road projected or under construction	Level crossing/Toll	Toll
Lerwick 14hrs	Car ferry route with journey time	Airport with scheduled services	
	Railway line and station	Heliport	
	Railway tunnel	Canal / dry canal / canal tunnel	
	Built up area	**Peterhead** Primary route destination	
	Town / Village / Other settlement		
	County / Unitary Authority boundary	Spot height (metres)	468
	Woodland	Summit height (metres)	491
	Beach	Lake / Dam / River / Waterfall	
8 20	National Grid reference	52 Page continuation number	

More details of the places of interest shown on the mapping can be found on pages 44-47

i / i Tourist information office (all year / seasonal)	Battlefield	Major sports venue
Preserved railway	Castle	Motor racing circuit
m Ancient monument	Garden	Wildlife park or Zoo
Ecclesiastical building	Country park	Other interesting feature
Historic house (with or without garden)	Nature reserve	Golf course
Museum / Art gallery	Theme park	(NTS) National Trust for Scotland
Factory shop village	Racecourse	

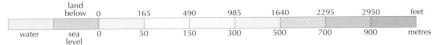

land below	0	165	490	985	1640	2295	2950	feet
water	sea level 0	50	150	300	500	700	900	metres

SCALE: 4 miles to 1 inch approx (10 km to 4 cm)

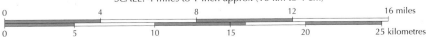

0		4		8		12		16 miles
0	5		10		15		20	25 kilometres

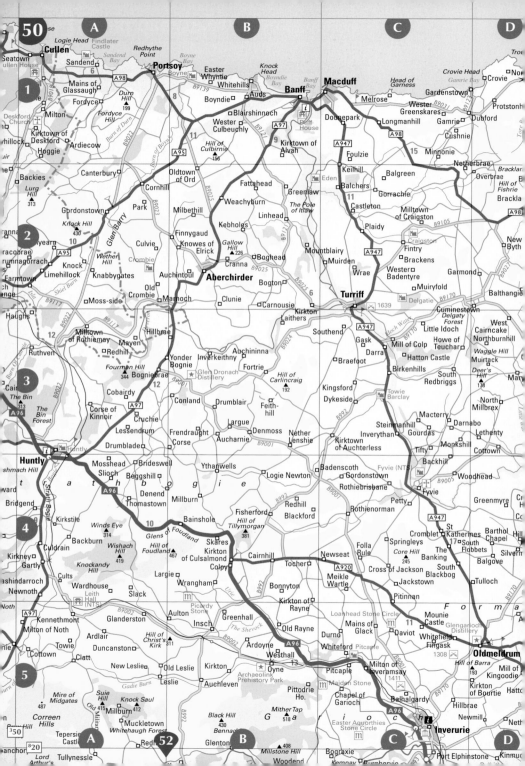

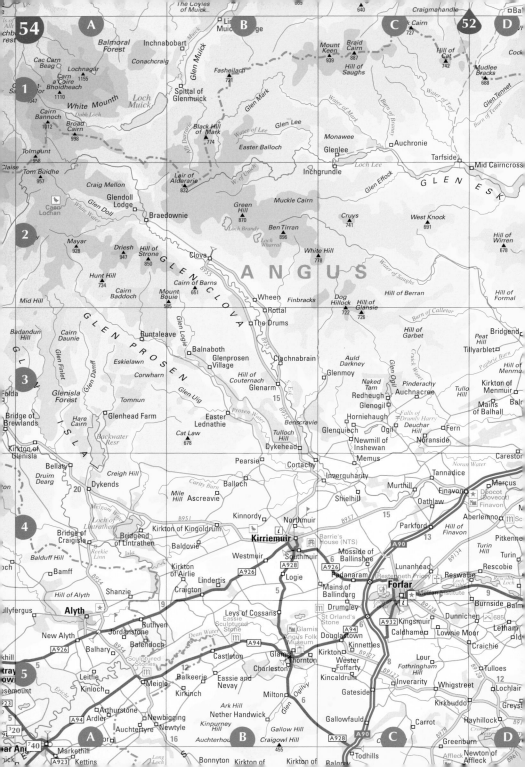

General abbreviations

All	Alley	Conv	Convent	Gdn	Garden	Ms	Mews	Sec	Secondary
Allot	Allotments	Cor	Corner	Gdns	Gardens	Mt	Mount	Shop	Shopping
Amb	Ambulance	Coron	Coroners	Govt	Government	Mus	Museum	Sq	Square
App	Approach	Cors	Corners	Gra	Grange	N	North	St.	Saint
Arc	Arcade	Cotts	Cottages	Grd	Ground	NT	National	St	Street
Av/Ave	Avenue	Cov	Covered	Grds	Grounds		Trust	Sta	Station
Bdy	Broadway	Crem	Crematorium	Grn	Green	Nat	National	Sts	Streets
Bk	Bank	Cres	Crescent	Grns	Greens	PH	Public House	Sub	Subway
Bldgs	Buildings	Ct	Court	Gro	Grove	PO	Post Office	Swim	Swimming
Boul	Boulevard	Cts	Courts	Gros	Groves	Par	Parade	TA	Territorial
Bowl	Bowling	Ctyd	Courtyard	Gt	Great	Pas	Passage		Army
Br/Bri	Bridge	Dep	Depot	Ho	House	Pav	Pavilion	TH	Town Hall
C of E	Church of	Dev	Development	Hos	Houses	Pk	Park	Tenn	Tennis
	England	Dr	Drive	Hosp	Hospital	Pl	Place	Ter	Terrace
Cath	Cathedral	Dws	Dwellings	Hts	Heights	Pol	Police	Thea	Theatre
Cem	Cemetery	E	East	Ind	Industrial	Prec	Precinct	Trd	Trading
Cen	Central,	Ed	Education	Int	International	Prim	Primary	Twr	Tower
	Centre	Elec	Electricity	Junct	Junction	Prom	Promenade	Twrs	Towers
Cft	Croft	Embk	Embankment	La	Lane	Pt	Point	Uni	University
Cfts	Crofts	Est	Estate	Las	Lanes	Quad	Quadrant	Up	Upper
Ch	Church	Ex	Exchange	Lib	Library	RC	Roman	Vil	Villa, Villas
Chyd	Churchyard	Exhib	Exhibition	Lo	Lodge		Catholic	Vw	View
Cin	Cinema	FB	Footbridge	Lwr	Lower	Rd	Road	W	West
Circ	Circus	FC	Football Club	Mag	Magistrates	Rds	Roads	Wd	Wood
Cl/Clo	Close	Fld	Field	Mans	Mansions	Rec	Recreation	Wds	Woods
Co	County	Flds	Fields	Mem	Memorial	Res	Reservoir	Wf	Wharf
Coll	College	Fm	Farm	Mid	Middle	Ri	Rise	Wk	Walk
Comm	Community	Gall	Gallery	Mkt	Market	S	South	Wks	Works
Comn	Common	Gar	Garage	Mkts	Markets	Sch	School	Yd	Yard

District abbreviations

Bield.	Bieldside	Dane.	Danestone
Br.Don	Bridge of Don	Kings.	Kingswells
Bucks.	Bucksburn	Newt.	Newtonhill
Co.Bay	Cove Bay	Port.	Portlethen

Post town abbreviations

Mill.	Milltimber
Peter.	Peterculter
Stone.	Stonehaven
Westh.	Westhill

This index contains streets that are not named on the map due to insufficient space. For each of these cases the nearest street that does appear on the map is also listed in *italics*.

Street	Page	Grid
Abbey La. (Torry) AB11	25	E4
Abbey Pl. AB11	25	E4
Abbey Rd. AB11	25	E4
Abbey Sq. AB11	25	E4
Abbots Pl. AB12	30	B1
Abbotsford La. AB11	24	B4
Abbotsford Pl. AB11	24	B4
Ferryhill Rd.		
Abbotshall Cres. (Cults) AB15	28	A2
Abbotshall Dr. (Cults) AB15	28	A2
Abbotshall Gdns. (Cults) AB15	28	A2
Abbotshall Pl. (Cults) AB15	28	A2
Abbotshall Rd. (Cults) AB15	28	B1
Abbotshall Ter. (Cults) AB15	28	A2
Abbotshall Wk. (Cults) AB15	28	A2
Abbotswell Cres. AB12	30	B1
Abbotswell Dr. AB12	30	A1
Abbotswell Rd. AB12	30	C1
Aberdeen Airport (Dyce) AB21	6	D4
Aberdeen Mkt. AB11	24	C2
Union St.		
Aberdeen Offshore Technology Pk. (Br.Don) AB23	11	G5
Aberdeen Science & Technology Pk. (Br.Don) AB22	10	C6
Aberdon Ct. AB24	14	C3
Coningham Ter.		
Aberdon Ho. Ct. AB24	14	C3
Coningham Rd.		
Abergeldie Rd. AB10	23	H5
Abergeldie Ter. AB10	23	H5
Aboyne Gdns. AB10	29	F1
Aboyne Pl. AB10	29	F2
Aboyne Rd. AB10	29	F2
Aboyne Ter. AB10	29	G2
Academy St. AB11	5	C3
Acorn Pl. (Port.) AB12	38	D5
Adelphi AB11	5	D2
Adelphi La. AB11 *Adelphi*	24	C2
Advocates Rd. AB24	15	E6
Affleck Pl. AB11	24	B3
Marywell St.		
Affleck St. AB11	5	C3
Airside Business Pk. (Dyce) AB21	6	C3
Airyhall Av. AB15	22	C6
Airyhall Cres. AB15	22	C6
Airyhall Dr. AB15	22	C6
Airyhall Gdns. AB15	22	D6
Airyhall Pl. AB15	22	D6
Airyhall Rd. AB15	28	C1
Airyhall Ter. AB15	22	D6
Albert La. AB25	23	G3
Albert Pl. AB25	4	A2
Albert Quay AB11	5	E3
Albert St. AB25	4	A2
Albert Ter. AB10	4	A3
Albert Wk. AB10	23	H3
Albert Ter.		
Albury Gdns. AB11	24	B4
Albury Rd.		
Albury Mans. AB11	24	B4
Albury Rd.		
Albury Pl. AB11	24	B4
Albury Rd. AB11	24	A4
Albyn Gro. AB10	4	A3
Albyn La. AB10	4	A3
Albyn Pl. AB10	4	A3
Albyn Ter. AB10	4	A3
Alder Dr. (Port.) AB12	38	C5
Alexander Dr. AB24	14	B2
Alexander Ter. AB24	14	B3
Alford La. AB10	4	B3
Alford Rd. AB10	24	A3
Albyn Pl.		
Allan St. AB10	23	H4
Allenvale Gdns. AB10	24	A6
Allenvale Rd. AB10	24	A6
Allison Cl. (Co.Bay) AB12	30	D5
Alma Rd. AB23	11	F6
Altens Fm. Rd. (Nigg) AB12	30	D2
Altens Ind. Est. AB12	30	C4
Altonrea Gdns. (Dyce) AB21	7	G3
Anderson Av. AB24	14	A3
Anderson Dr. AB15	23	E4
Anderson Dr. (Newt.), Stone. AB39	41	E4
Anderson Rd. AB24	13	H3
Angusfield Av. AB15	22	D3
Angusfield La. AB15	22	D3
Ann St. AB25	4	B1
Annat Bk. AB12	31	E5
Annfield Ter. AB10	23	G4
Arbroath La. AB12	30	B2
Arbroath Pl. AB12	30	C2
Arbroath Way AB12	30	B2
Ardarroch Cl. AB24	15	F5
Ardarroch Rd.		
Ardarroch Pl. AB24	15	F5
Ardarroch Rd. AB24	15	E5
Ardbeck Pl., Peter. AB14	33	E2
Ardlair Ter. (Dyce) AB21	7	G2
Argyll Cl. AB21	6	C5
Argyll Cres. AB25	23	G1
Argyll Pl. (Port.) AB12	39	E2
Argyll Pl. AB25	23	G1
Argyll Rd. (Dyce) AB21	6	C5
Arnage Cres. AB16	13	F6
Arnage Dr. AB16	13	E6
Arnage Gdns. AB16	13	F6
Arnage Pl. AB16	13	F6
Arnage Ter. AB16	13	F6
Arnhall Business Pk., Westh. AB32	17	E5
Arnhall Cres., Westh. AB32	17	F5
Arnhall Dr., Westh. AB32	17	F5
Arnot Pl. (Port.) AB12	39	G4
Arran Av. AB16	12	B6
Aryburn Row (Dyce) AB21	7	G3

Ash Ct. (Port.) AB12	38	C4
Ash Gro. (Port.) AB12	38	D5
Ash Pl. (Port.) AB12	38	D5
Ash-hill Dr. AB16	13	H5
Ash-hill Pl. AB16	14	A5
Rosehill Dr.		
Ash-hill Rd. AB16	14	A5
Ash-hill Way AB16	14	A5
Ashdale Cl., Westh. AB32	16	D4
Ashdale Ct., Westh. AB32	17	E4
Ashdale Dr.		
Ashdale Dr., Westh. AB32	17	E4
Ashfield Rd. (Cults) AB15	28	B2
Ashgrove Av. AB25	14	B5
Ashgrove Ct. AB25	14	A5
Ashgrove Gdns. N. AB16	13	G6
Ashgrove Gdns. S. AB16	13	G6
Ashgrove Pl. AB16	13	G6
Ashgrove Rd. AB25	14	B6
Ashgrove Rd. W. AB16	13	G6
Ashgrove Rd. W. AB25	13	G6
Ashley Gdns. AB10	23	G4
Ashley Gro. AB10	23	H4
Ashley La. AB10	23	G4
Ashley Pk. Dr. AB10	23	G4
Ashley Pk. La. AB10	23	H4
Ashley Pk. N. AB10	23	G4
Ashley Pk. S. AB10	23	H4
Ashley Rd. AB10	23	H4
Ashtown Pl. (Bucks.) AB21	12	B2
Newhills Av.		
Ashtown Wk. (Bucks.) AB21	12	B2
Ashvale Ct. AB10	24	A3
Cuparstone Row		
Ashvale Pl. AB10	4	A3
Ashwood Av. (Br.Don) AB22	10	B3
Ashwood Circle (Br.Don) AB22	10	B2
Ashwood Cres. (Br.Don) AB22	10	A3
Ashwood Dr. (Br.Don) AB22	10	B3
Ashwood Gdns. (Br.Don) AB22	10	B2
Ashwood Gra. (Br.Don) AB22	10	B3
Ashwood Ms. (Br.Don) AB22	10	B2
Ashwood Par. (Br.Don) AB22	10	A2
Ashwood Par. (Br.Don) AB22	10	B2
Ashwood Pk. (Br.Don) AB22	10	B3
Ashwood Pl. (Br.Don) AB22	10	A2
Ashwood Rd. (Br.Don) AB22	10	B2
Aspen Gro., Westh. AB32	16	C5
Aspen Way (Port.) AB12	38	D5
Auchinleck Cres. AB24	14	B2
Auchinleck Rd. AB24	14	B2
Auchinyell Gdns. AB10	29	F1
Auchinyell Rd. AB10	29	F1
Auchinyell Ter. AB10	29	F1
Auchlea Pl. AB16	22	A1
Auchlea Rd. AB16	22	A1
Auchlossan Ct. (Br.Don) AB22	14	D1
Davan Pk.		
Auchmill Rd. (Bucks.) AB21	12	D1
Auchmill Ter. (Bucks.) AB21	13	F2
Auchriny Circle (Bucks.) AB21	7	F6
Auckland Pl. AB24	15	E5
Merkland Pl.		
Auldearn Gdns. AB12	30	B2
Auldearn Pl. AB12	30	B2
Auldearn Rd. AB12	30	B2
Aulton Ct. AB24	15	F3
Avon Pl. (Dyce) AB21	7	F3
B		
Back Hilton Rd. AB25	14	B5
Back Wynd AB10	5	C2
Badentoy Av. (Badentoy Ind. Est.) AB12	38	B1
Badentoy Business Cen. (Port.) AB12	38	A1
Badentoy Cres. (Badentoy Ind. Est.) AB12	38	A1
Badentoy Pk. Ind. Est.	38	B1
Badentoy Pl. (Badentoy Ind. Est.) AB12	38	B1
Badentoy Rd. (Badentoy Ind. Est.) AB12	38	C2
Bailliieswell Gro. (Bield.) AB15	27	F3
Baillieswells Cres. (Bield.) AB15	27	F3
Baillieswells Dr. (Bield.) AB15	27	F3
Baillieswells Pl. (Bield.) AB15	27	F3
Baillieswells Rd. (Bield.) AB15	27	F3

Baillieswells Ter. (Bield.) AB15	27	F3
Bairds Brae (Cults) AB15	28	C1
Baker Pl. AB25	24	A1
Baker St.		
Baker St. AB25	4	B1
Balfron Pl. AB15	22	D2
Balgownie Brae (Br.Don) AB22	14	C1
Balgownie Ct. AB24	15	E3
Balgownie Cres. (Br.Don) AB23	15	E1
Balgownie Dr. (Br.Don) AB22	14	B1
Balgownie Gdns. (Br.Don) AB22	14	C1
Balgownie Pl. (Br.Don) AB22	14	B1
Balgownie Rd. (Br.Don) AB22	14	D1
Balgownie Rd. (Br.Don) AB23	15	E1
Balgownie Way (Br.Don) AB22	14	B1
Balloch Way AB21	7	G2
Balmoral Ct. AB10	24	A5
South Mile End		
Balmoral Pl. AB10	23	H5
Balmoral Rd. AB10	24	A5
Balmoral Ter. AB10	23	H5
Balnagask Av. AB11	25	F5
Balnagask Circle		
Balnagask Circle AB11	25	F5
Balnagask Pl. AB11	25	F4
Balnagask Rd. AB11	25	E5
Balnagask Wk. AB11	25	E5
Farquhar Rd.		
Baltic Pl. AB11	25	E2
Baltic St. AB11	5	E2
Bank St. AB11	24	B4
Bank St. (Woodside) AB24	14	A3
Bankhead Av. (Bucks.) AB21	12	B1
Bankhead Ind. Est. (Bucks.) AB21	12	C1
Bankhead Rd. (Bucks.) AB21	8	C6
Bannerman Pl. AB16	12	D3
Bannermill Pl. AB24	24	D1
Beach Boul.		
Bannermill St. AB11	24	D1
Cotton St.		
Barbour Brae (Br.Don) AB22	10	B6
Barclayhill Pl. (Port.) AB12	39	E2
Barkmill Rd. AB25	14	B5
Ashgrove Rd.		
Barra Wk. AB16	22	A1
Barringer La., Westh. AB32	17	F4
Barron St. AB24	14	B3
Sandilands Dr.		
Barrowstone Pl. AB16	22	A1
Derbeth Cres.		
Barvas Wk. AB16	12	B6
Bath St. AB11	24	B2
Windmill Brae		
Battock Pl. AB11	24	D5
Baxter Ct. AB11	25	F4
Baxter Pl.		
Baxter Pl. AB11	25	F4
Baxter St. AB11	25	E4
Bayview Ct. AB24	15	F4
Bayview Rd. AB15	23	F3
Bayview Rd. S. AB15	23	F4
Beach Boul. AB24	5	E1
Beachview Ct. AB24	15	F3
Beaconhill Rd., Mill. AB13	26	D5
Beaconsfield Pl. AB15	23	F3
Beattie Av. AB25	14	B5
Beattie Pl. AB25	14	B5
Elder Pl.		
Bedford Av. AB24	14	C4
Bedford Pl. AB24	14	C5
Bedford Rd. AB24	14	C5
Beech Rd. AB16	13	F5
Beech Rd., Westh. AB32	16	D5
Beechgrove Av. AB15	23	G2
Beechgrove Ct. AB15	23	G2
Beechgrove Ter.		
Beechgrove Gdns. AB15	23	G1
Beechgrove Pl. AB15	23	G2
Beechgrove Ter. AB15	23	G2
Beechhill Gdns. AB15	22	D6
Beechwood Av. AB16	13	H6
Beechwood Cl., Westh. AB32	16	C5
Beechwood Gdns.		
Beechwood Ct. AB16	13	G6
Castleton Dr.		
Beechwood Gdns., Westh. AB32	16	C5
Beechwood Pl. AB16	13	H5
Beechwood Pl., Westh. AB32	16	C4

Beechwood Rd. AB16	13	H5
Beechwood Wk. AB16	13	H5
Belgrave Ter. AB25	4	A2
Bellenden Wk., Mill. AB13	26	A6
Bellfield Rd. AB16	12	D6
Bellfield Rd. (Br.Don) AB23	11	E6
Belmont Gdns. AB25	14	B5
Belmont Rd. AB25	14	C5
Belmont St. AB10	5	C2
Belmuir Gdns. (Dyce) AB21	7	F2
Belrorie Circle (Dyce) AB21	7	G2
Belvidere Cres. AB25	4	A2
Belvidere La. (Cults) AB15	28	A3
Belvidere Rd. (Cults) AB15	27	H3
Belvidere St. AB25	4	A1
Benbecula Rd. AB16	12	B6
Berneray Pl. AB16	22	A1
Berry St. AB25	5	D1
Berryden Business Pk. AB25	14	C6
Berryden Rd.		
Berryden Rd. AB25	14	C6
Berryhill Pl. (Newt.), Stone. AB39	40	D4
Berrymoss Ct. (Dyce) AB21	7	G2
Balloch Way		
Berrymuir Pl. (Port.) AB12	38	C5
Berrymuir Rd. (Port.) AB12	38	C5
Berrymuir Wynd (Port.) AB12	38	C5
Berrywell Gdns. (Dyce) AB21	7	F2
Berrywell Pl. (Dyce) AB21	7	F2
Berrywell Rd. (Dyce) AB21	7	F2
Berrywell Wk. (Dyce) AB21	7	F2
Bervie Brow AB12	30	D5
Bethany Gdns. AB11	24	A4
Bethlin Ms. (Kings.) AB15	18	D4
Bettridge Rd. (Newt.), Stone. AB39	41	E4
Binghill Cres., Mill. AB13	26	B5
Binghill Dr., Mill. AB13	26	B4
Binghill Hedges, Mill. AB13	26	B4
Binghill Pk., Mill. AB13	26	C5
Binghill Rd., Mill. AB13	26	C4
Binghill Rd. N., Mill. AB13	26	B4
Binghill Rd. W., Mill. AB13	26	B4
Birch Av., Westh. AB32	16	D5
Birch Rd. AB16	13	H5
Rowan Rd.		
Birchfield Pl. (Co.Bay) AB12	37	G1
Redwood Cres.		
Birkhall Par. AB16	13	E5
Birkhall Pl. AB16	13	E5
Bishopsloch Row (Dyce) AB21	7	G3
Blackburn Pl. (Old Aberdeen) AB24	14	D4
High St.		
Blackfriars St. AB25	4	C1
Blackhills Ct., Westh. AB32	16	C4
Blackhills Pl.		
Blackhills Pl., Westh. AB32	16	C4
Blackhills Way, Westh. AB32	16	C4
Blackhills Pl.		
Blacklaws Brae, Westh. AB32	16	D2
Blackness Av. (Altens Ind. Est.) AB12	31	F4
Blackness Rd. (Altens Ind. Est.) AB12	31	F4
Blacks La. AB11	5	E3
Blacksmiths Cft. (Bucks.) AB21	13	E2
Cairnfield Pl.		
Blackthorn Cres. AB16	13	H5
Blaikies Quay AB11	5	E2
Bleachfield Rd. (Br.Don) AB22	10	C6
Silverburn Rd.		
Blenheim La. AB25	23	G2
Blenheim Pl. AB25	23	G2
Bloomfield Rd. AB10	24	A5
Bloomfield Pl. AB10	24	A4
Bloomfield Rd. AB10	24	A5
Boa Vista Pl. AB24	14	D5
Spital		
Bob Cooney Ct. AB25	14	C6
Bodachra Path (Br.Don) AB22	10	C6
Bodachra Pl.		
Bodachra Pl. (Br.Don) AB22	10	C6
Bodachra Rd. (Br.Don) AB22	10	C6
Boddie Pl. AB24	15	E6
Bon Accord Cres. AB11	4	C3
Bon Accord Cres. La. AB11	24	B3
Bon Accord Cres.		
Bon Accord La. AB11	4	C3
Bon Accord Sq. AB11	4	C3
Bon Accord St. AB11	4	C3
Bon Accord Ter. AB11	4	B3

Bonnymuir Pl. AB15	23	G1
Bonnyview Dr. AB16	12	D3
Bonnyview Pl. AB16	12	D3
Bonnyview Rd. AB16	12	D3
Bonnyview Dr.		
Booth Pl. (Bucks.) AB21	12	C1
Kingsway		
Borrowstone Pl. AB16	12	C6
Sheddocksley Dr.		
Boswell Av. (Port.) AB12	38	C3
Boswell Rd. (Port.) AB12	38	C3
Boswell Wk. (Port.) AB12	38	C3
Boswell Way (Port.) AB12	38	C3
Boswell Wynd (Port.) AB12	38	C3
Bourtree Av. (Port.) AB12	38	C5
Boyd Orr Av. AB12	30	A4
Boyd Orr Cl. AB12	30	A4
Boyd Orr Pl. AB12	29	H4
Boyd Orr Wk. AB12	29	H4
Bracken Rd. (Port.) AB12	38	D3
Bradley Ter. AB24	14	C3
Braecroft Av., Westh. AB32	17	E4
Braecroft Cres., Westh. AB32	17	E4
Braecroft Dr., Westh. AB32	17	E4
Braefoot Rd. AB16	14	A5
Braehead (Br.Don) AB22	10	D6
Glashieburn Way		
Braehead Ter., Mill. AB13	26	B5
Braehead Way (Br.Don) AB22	10	C6
Braemar Pl. AB10	23	H5
Braeside Av. AB15	29	E1
Braeside Pl. AB15	22	D6
Braeside Ter. AB15	29	E1
Bramble Brae AB16	13	G4
Bramble Ct. (Port.) AB12	38	D5
Bramble Pl. (Port.) AB12	38	D5
Bramble Way (Port.) AB12	38	D5
Brander Pl. (Dane.) AB24	14	A1
Brebner Cres. AB16	12	D4
Brebner Ter. AB16	12	D4
Brebner's Ct. AB11	24	C2
Justice St.		
Brent Rd. (Dyce) AB21	6	D4
Bressay Brae AB15	22	A1
Brewery La. AB24	14	D4
High St.		
Bridge of Dee AB10	29	H1
Bridge of Dee Ct. AB10	29	H1
Bridge of Don AB24	15	F2
Bridge of Don Ind. Est. AB23	11	E5
Bridge Pl. AB11	24	B2
Bridge St.		
Bridge St. AB11	5	C2
Bridge St. (Woodside) AB24	13	H3
Great Northern Rd.		
Brierfield Rd. AB16	13	H5
Brierfield Ter. AB16	13	G5
Brig o' Balgownie AB24	15	E1
Bright St. AB11	24	B5
Brighton Gra., Peter. AB14	32	D3
Brighton Pl. AB10	23	G4
Brighton Pl., Peter. AB14	32	D3
Brimmond Ct. AB11	25	F5
Balnagask Circle		
Brimmond Ct., Westh. AB32	16	D5
Brimmond Cres., Westh. AB32	16	D5
Brimmond Dr., Westh. AB32	16	D5
Brimmond La., Westh. AB32	16	D5
Brimmond Pl. AB11	24	D5
Brimmond Pl., Westh. AB32	16	D5
Brimmond Vw. (Bucks.) AB21	8	B5
Brimmond Wk., Westh. AB32	16	D5
Brimmond Way, Westh. AB32	16	D5
Brimmondside (Bucks.) AB21	12	A2
Broad St. AB10	5	D2
Broaddykes Av. (Kings.) AB15	18	D4
Broaddykes Cl. (Kings.) AB15	18	D4
Broaddykes Cres. (Kings.) AB15	18	D5
Broaddykes Dr. (Kings.) AB15	18	C5
Broaddykes Pl. (Kings.) AB15	18	C4
Broaddykes Vw. (Kings.) AB15	18	D5
Broaddykes Way (Kings.) AB15	18	C5
Broaddykes Dr.		
Broadfold Dr. (Br.Don) AB23	11	E6
Broadfold Rd. (Br.Don) AB23	11	E5
Broadfold Ter. (Br.Don) AB23	11	E6
Gordon Pl.		
Broadhaven Rd. (Port.) AB12	39	G4
Broadlands Gdns., Westh. AB32	16	B4
Old Skene Rd.		
Broadstraik Av., Westh. AB32	16	B5
Broadstraik Brae, Westh. AB32	16	B5
Broadstraik Dr., Westh. AB32	16	B5
Broadstraik Gdns., Westh. AB32	16	A4
Broadstraik Pl., Westh. AB32	16	B5
Brodiach Ct., Westh. AB32	17	F4
Brodinch Pl. AB16	12	D6
Brodinch Rd. AB16	12	D6
Brooke Cres. (Br.Don) AB23	11	E4
Broom Pk. AB15	27	H2
Broomfield Pk. (Port.) AB12	38	C4
Broomfield Rd. (Port.) AB12	38	C4
Broomhill Av. AB10	23	H6
Broomhill Pk. AB10	23	H5
Broomhill Rd.		
Broomhill Pl. AB10	23	H6
Broomhill Rd. AB10	23	H5
Broomhill Ter. AB10	23	H6
Brough Pl. AB25	14	A5
Carnie Dr.		
Brown St. AB24	14	A3
Bruce Ho. AB15	22	B3
Hazlehead Rd.		
Bruce Wk. AB12	30	C3
Brucklay Ct. (Dyce) AB21	7	G3
Brunswick Pl. AB11	24	B5
Bruntland Ct. (Port.) AB12	38	D4
Bruntland Pl. (Port.) AB12	39	E4
Bruntland Rd. (Port.) AB12	38	D4
Buchan Pl. AB11	25	F5
Buchan Rd. AB11	25	F5
Buchan Rd. (Dyce) AB21	6	C3
Buchan Ter. AB11	25	F5
Buchanan Gdns. AB12	30	B3
Buchanan Pl. AB12	30	B3
Buchanan Rd. AB12	30	B3
Buckie Av. (Br.Don) AB22	10	A5
Buckie Cl. (Br.Don) AB22	10	A5
Buckie Cres. (Br.Don) AB22	10	A5
Buckie Gro. (Br.Don) AB22	10	B5
Buckie Rd. (Br.Don) AB22	10	A5
Buckie Wk. (Br.Don) AB22	10	A5
Buckie Wynd (Br.Don) AB22	10	A5
Bucklerburn Cl., Peter. AB14	32	C1
Bucklerburn Dr., Peter. AB14	32	D2
Bucklerburn Pk., Peter. AB14	32	D2
Bucklerburn Pl., Peter. AB14	32	D2
Bucklerburn Rd., Peter. AB14	32	D1
Bucklerburn Vw., Peter. AB14	32	D1
Bucklerburn Wynd, Peter. AB14	32	C2
Bunstane Ter. (Co.Bay) AB12	37	G1
Spark Ter.		
Bunzeach Pl. (Dyce) AB21	7	G2
Ardlair Ter.		
Burnbank Pl. AB11	25	E5
Burnbank Ter. AB11	25	E5
Burnbanks Village (Co. Bay) AB12	31	F4
Burnbrae Av. AB16	22	C1
Burnbrae Cres. AB16	22	C1
Burnbrae Rd. AB16	22	C1
Burnbutts Cres. (Co.Bay) AB12	37	G1
Burndale Rd. (Bucks.) AB21	8	C6
Burnett Pl. AB24	14	B4
Burnieboozle Cres. AB15	22	B5
Burnieboozle Pl. AB15	22	C5
Burns Gdns. AB15	23	F4
Burns Rd. AB15	23	F4
Burnside Dr. (Dyce) AB21	7	G4
Burnside Dr. (Br.Don) AB23	11	E6
Burnside Gdns. (Port.) AB12	39	E3
Burnside Gdns. AB25	23	G1
Burnside Rd. (Dyce) AB21	7	G4
Burnside Rd., Peter. AB14	32	D4
Bush, The, Peter. AB14	32	D3
Bute Way AB16	22	A1
Bydand Pl. (Br.Don) AB23	11	E4
Byron Av. AB16	13	E5
Byron Cres. AB16	12	D4
Byron Pk. AB16	13	E5
Springhill Ter.		
Byron Sq. AB16	13	E4
Byron Ter. AB16	12	D5

C

Cadenhead Pl. AB25	14	B5
Cadenhead Rd. AB25	14	B5
Caiesdykes Cres. AB12	30	A3
Caiesdykes Dr. AB12	30	A2
Caiesdykes Rd. AB12	30	A3
Cairn Cres. (Cults) AB15	27	G3
Cairn Gdns. (Cults) AB15	27	G3
Cairn Pk. (Cults) AB15	27	G3
Cairn Rd. (Bield.) AB15	27	G3
Cairn Wk. (Cults) AB15	27	G3
Cairnaquheen Gdns. AB15	23	F1
Cairnaquheen Pl. AB15	23	F2
Cairnaquheen Gdns.		
Cairncry Av. AB16	13	H5
Cairncry Ct. AB16	13	G5
Cairncry Cres. AB16	14	A5
Cairncry Rd. AB16	13	H5
Cairncry Ter. AB16	13	H5
Cairnfield Circle (Bucks.) AB21	13	E1
Cairnfield Cres. (Bucks.) AB21	13	E2
Cairnfield Gdns. (Bucks.) AB21	13	E2
Auchinleck Rd.		
Cairnfield Pl. AB15	23	G1
Cairnfield Pl. (Bucks.) AB21	13	E2
Cairnfold Rd. (Br.Don) AB22	14	D1
Cairngorm Cres. AB12	30	B2
Cairngorm Dr. AB12	30	A2
Cairngorm Gdns. AB12	30	B2
Cairngorm Pl. AB12	30	A2
Cairngorm Rd. AB12	30	H2
Cairngrassie Circle (Port.) AB12	38	C5
Cairngrassie Dr. (Port.) AB12	38	C5
Cairnhill Dr. (Newt.), Stone. AB39	40	C4
Cairnhill Pl. (Newt.), Stone. AB39	40	C4
Cairnhill Rd. (Newt.), Stone. AB39	40	C4
Cairnhillock Pl. (Bucks.) AB21	12	B3
Newhills Av.		
Cairnie Vw., Westh. AB32	16	D3
Cairnlee Av. E. (Cults) AB15	27	G3
Cairnlee Cres. N. AB15	27	G3
Cairnlee Cres. S. (Cults) AB15	27	G3
Cairnlee Pk. (Bield.) AB15	27	F3
Cairnlee Rd. (Bield.) AB15	27	F3
Cairnlee Rd. E. (Cults) AB15	27	G2
Cairnlee Ter. (Bield.) AB15	27	F3
Cairnside (Cults) AB15	27	G3
Cairnton Ct., Westh. AB32	17	E4
Ashdale Dr.		
Cairnvale Cres. AB12	30	A2
Cairnvale Ter. AB12	30	A2
Cairnview Cres. AB16	13	H5
Cairnwell Av. AB16	13	E6
Cairnwell Dr. (Port.) AB12	38	D4
Cairnwell Pl. AB16	13	E5
Cairnwell Pl. AB16	13	E5
Caledonian Brae AB11	24	B4
Ferryhill Rd.		
Caledonian Ct. AB11	24	B4
Ferryhill Ter.		
Caledonian La. AB11	24	B4
Caledonian Pl.		
Caledonian Pl. AB11	24	B4
Callum Cres. (Kings.) AB15	18	C3
Callum Pk. (Kings.) AB15	18	C3
Callum Path (Kings.) AB15	18	C3
Callum Wynd (Kings.) AB15	18	C3
Calsayseat Rd. AB25	14	C6
Cameron Av. (Br.Don) AB23	10	D6
Cameron Dr. (Br.Don) AB23	10	D6
Cameron Pl. (Br.Don) AB23	11	E6
Cameron Rd. (Br.Don) AB23	10	D6
Cameron St. (Br.Don) AB23	11	E6
Cameron Ter. (Br.Don) AB23	10	D6
Cameron Way (Br.Don) AB23	10	D6
Cammach Circle (Port.) AB12	38	C5
Camperdown Rd. AB15	23	F1
Campsie Pl. AB15	22	D2
Campus One (Br.Don) AB22	14	C1
Campus Three (Br.Don) AB22	14	C1
Campus Two (Br.Don) AB22	14	C1
Canal Pl. AB24	14	D6
Canal Rd. AB25	14	D6
Canal St. AB24	14	D6
Canal St. (Woodside) AB24	14	A2
Canal Ter. AB24	13	H2
Candlemakers La. AB25	24	B1
Loch St.		
Caperstown Cres. AB16	13	F4
Carden Pl. AB10	23	G3

Name	Page	Grid
Carden Ter. AB10	4	A3
Cardens Knowe (Br.Don) AB22	10	D6
Glashieburn Way		
Carlin Ter. (Dyce) AB21	7	G2
Netherview Av.		
Carlton Pl. AB15	23	F2
Carmelite La. AB11	24	C2
Wapping St.		
Carmelite St. AB11	24	C2
Wapping St.		
Carnegie Cres. AB15	23	E3
Carnegie Gdns. AB15	23	E3
Carnegies Brae AB10	24	C2
Flourmill La.		
Carnie Dr. AB25	14	A5
Carnie Gdns. AB25	14	A5
Carnie Dr.		
Carnoustie Cres. (Br.Don) AB22	10	C5
Carnoustie Gdns. (Br.Don) AB22	10	C5
Carnoustie Cres.		
Caroline Apartments AB25	24	A1
Forbes St.		
Caroline Pl. AB25	24	A1
Hutcheon St.		
Carron Pl. AB16	13	E5
Cassie Cl. (Co.Bay) AB12	30	D6
Castle St. AB11	5	D2
Castle Ter. AB11	5	E2
Castlegate AB11	24	C2
Justice St.		
Castlehill AB11	24	D1
Hanover St.		
Castleton Ct. AB16	13	G6
Castleton Dr.		
Castleton Cres. AB16	13	G6
Castleton Dr. AB16	13	G6
Castleton La. AB16	13	G6
Castleton Cres.		
Castleton Pk. AB16	13	G6
Castleton Cres.		
Castleton Way AB16	13	G6
Castleton Cres.		
Catherine St. AB25	4	C1
Catto Cres. (Co.Bay) AB12	31	E6
Catto Wk. (Co.Bay) AB12	31	E6
Cattofield Gdns. AB25	14	B5
Cattofield Pl. AB25	14	B5
Cattofield Ter. AB25	14	B5
Causewayend AB25	14	D6
Cava Cl. AB15	22	A1
Cedar Pl. AB25	14	B6
Centre Point (Br.Don) AB23	11	E4
Chanonry AB24	14	D3
Chapel Ct. AB11	24	D2
Justice St.		
Chapel Rd. (Newt.), Stone. AB39	41	E4
Chapel St. AB10	4	B2
Chapman Pl. AB16	13	E3
Provost Rust Dr.		
Chapman Wk. AB16	13	E3
Provost Rust Dr.		
Chapman Way AB16	13	E3
Howes Cres.		
Charles Pl. AB25	14	D6
Charles St.		
Charles St. AB25	14	D6
Charleston Av. (Co. Bay) AB12	37	E2
Charleston Cres. (Co. Bay) AB12	37	E1
Charleston Dr. (Co. Bay) AB12	36	D2
Charleston Gdns. (Co. Bay) AB12	37	E1
Charleston Gro. (Co. Bay) AB12	36	D1
Charleston Pl. (Co. Bay) AB12	36	D2
Charleston Rd. (Co. Bay) AB12	30	C6
Charleston Way (Co. Bay) AB12	37	E1
Charlestown Circle (Co. Bay) AB12	37	E2
Charlestown Wk. (Co. Bay) AB12	37	E1
Charlotte Gdns. AB25	4	C1
Charlotte Pl. AB25	4	C1
Charlotte St. AB25	4	C1
Chattan Pl. AB10	23	H4
Cherry Rd. AB16	13	H5
Chestnut Row AB25	14	B6
Cheyne Rd. AB24	15	E3
Church La. (Bucks.) AB21	12	B1
Inverurie Rd.		
Church St. AB11	5	E2
Church St. (Woodside) AB24	14	A3
Church Wk. AB24	14	D4
High St.		
Churchill Rd. AB23	11	F6
Claremont Gdns. AB10	23	H4
Claremont Gro. AB10	23	H4
Claremont Pl. AB10	23	H4
Claremont St. AB10	23	H4
Clarence St. AB11	5	E2
Clarke St. AB16	13	G3
Clarks La. AB24	15	E3
Clashbog Pl. (Bucks.) AB21	12	B2
Clashfarquhar Cres. (Port.) AB12	38	C3
Clashieknowe (Br.Don) AB22	10	D6
Scotstown Rd.		
Clashnettie Pl. (Dyce) AB21	7	G3
Clashrodney Av. (Co.Bay) AB12	37	F1
Clashrodney Rd. (Co.Bay) AB12	37	F1
Clashrodney Wk. (Co.Bay) AB12	37	F1
Clashrodney Way (Co.Bay) AB12	37	F1
Claymore Av. (Port.) AB12	39	E2
Claymore Av. (Br.Don) AB23	11	G4
Claymore Dr. (Br.Don) AB23	11	G4
Clerk Maxwell Cres. AB12	29	H4
Cliff Pk. (Cults) AB15	28	B2
Cliff Vw. (Newt.), Stone. AB39	40	D4
Clifton Ct. AB24	14	B3
Great Northern Rd.		
Clifton La. AB24	14	B4
Clifton Pl. AB24	14	B4
Clifton Rd. AB24	13	H3
Cloghill Pl. AB16	22	B1
Sheddocksley Dr.		
Clova Cres. (Kings.) AB15	18	C4
Clova Pk. (Kings.) AB15	18	C4
Clover Meadow, Westh. AB32	16	B4
Cloverdale Ct. (Bucks.) AB21	12	B1
Sclattie Pk.		
Cloverfield Cl. (Bucks.) AB21	12	B1
Cloverfield Ct. (Bucks.) AB21	12	A1
Cloverfield Gdns. (Bucks.) AB21	12	B1
Cloverfield Pl. (Bucks.) AB21	12	A1
Cloverhill Cres. (Br.Don) AB22	10	C6
Cloverhill Rd. (Br.Don) AB23	11	E6
Clunie Pl. AB16	13	E5
Clyde St. AB11	5	E3
Coldstone Av. (Kings.) AB15	18	C4
Coll Wk. AB16	22	A1
College Bounds AB24	14	D4
College St. AB11	5	C3
Collieston Av. (Br.Don) AB22	10	C4
Collieston Circle (Br.Don) AB22	10	C5
Collieston Cres. (Br.Don) AB22	10	D4
Collieston Dr. (Br.Don) AB22	10	D5
Collieston Path (Br.Don) AB22	10	C4
Collieston Pl. (Br.Don) AB22	10	C5
Collieston St. (Br.Don) AB22	10	D5
Collieston Way (Br.Don) AB22	10	D4
Colonsay Cres. AB16	22	A1
Colsea Rd. (Co.Bay) AB12	37	G1
Colsea Sq. (Co.Bay) AB12	37	G1
Colsea Rd.		
Colsea Ter. (Co.Bay) AB12	37	G1
Colthill Circle, Mill. AB13	26	B5
Colthill Cres., Mill. AB13	26	B4
Colthill Dr., Mill. AB13	26	B5
Colthill Rd., Mill. AB13	26	B4
Colville Pl. AB24	15	E6
Commerce St. AB11	5	E2
Commercial Quay AB11	5	E3
Concert Ct. AB10	24	C2
Broad St.		
Concraig Gdns. (Kings.) AB15	19	E3
Concraig Pl. (Kings.) AB15	19	E3
Conference Way (Br.Don) AB23	11	F5
Coningham Gdns. AB24	14	C3
Coningham Rd. AB24	14	C3
Coningham Ter. AB24	14	C3
Constitution Ct. AB24	24	D1
Constitution St.		
Constitution La. AB24	24	D1
Wales St.		
Constitution St. AB24	5	E1
Contlaw Brae, Mill. AB13	26	B5
Contlaw Pl., Mill. AB13	26	B5
Contlaw Rd., Mill. AB13	26	A4
Cookston Rd. (Port.) AB12	38	D2
Corby Ter. (Dyce) AB21	7	G3
Cordyce Vw. (Dyce) AB21	7	E3
Cormorant Brae (Co. Bay) AB12	30	C5
Corndavon Ter. AB16	13	F6
Cornhill Ct. AB16	13	H5
Cornhill Dr. AB16	13	H5
Cornhill Gdns. AB16	13	H5
Cornhill Rd. AB25	13	H6
Cornhill Shopping Arc. AB16	13	G5
Cornhill Dr.		
Cornhill Sq. AB16	14	A5
Ash-hill Rd.		
Cornhill Ter. AB16	13	H5
Cornhill Way AB16	13	H6
Cornyhaugh Rd., Peter. AB14	32	C2
Coronation Ct., Peter. AB14	33	E3
Coronation Rd.		
Coronation Rd., Peter. AB14	33	E3
Correction Wynd AB10	24	C2
Schoolhill		
Corrennie Circle (Dyce) AB21	7	F1
Corse Av. (Kings.) AB15	18	C3
Corse Gdns. (Kings.) AB15	18	D3
Corse Wynd (Kings.) AB15	18	D3
Corsehill Gdns. (Br.Don) AB22	14	C1
Corthan Cres. AB12	30	B1
Corthan Dr. AB12	30	B1
Corthan Pl. AB12	30	B1
Corunna Rd. AB23	15	F1
Cothal Vw. AB21	7	E1
Cottage Brae AB10	23	H4
Cotton St. AB11	5	E1
Cottown of Balgownie AB23	15	E1
Coull Gdns. (Kings.) AB15	18	C4
Coull Gdns. (Br.Don) AB22	14	D1
Coull Grn. (Kings.) AB15	18	C4
Countesswells Av. AB15	22	B5
Countesswells Cres. AB15	22	B5
Countesswells Pl. AB15	22	C5
Countesswells Rd. AB15	22	D6
Countesswells Ter. AB15	22	C5
Courtyard, The (Cults) AB15	28	A3
Millden Rd.		
Cove Circle (Co.Bay) AB12	37	F1
Cove Cl. (Co.Bay) AB12	37	F1
Cove Ct. (Co.Bay) AB12	37	G1
Cove Cres. (Co.Bay) AB12	37	F2
Cove Gdns. (Co.Bay) AB12	37	F1
Cove Path (Co.Bay) AB12	37	G1
Cove Pl. (Co.Bay) AB12	37	G1
Cove Rd. (Co.Bay) AB12	37	F1
Cove Wk. (Co.Bay) AB12	37	F1
Cove Way (Co.Bay) AB12	37	F1
Cove Wynd (Co.Bay) AB12	37	F1
Covenanters Dr. AB12	30	B1
Covenanters Row AB12	30	A1
Cowan Pl. AB24	14	B2
Alexander Dr.		
Craibstone Av. (Bucks.) AB21	7	F6
Craibstone La. AB11	24	B4
Bon Accord St.		
Craig Gdns. (Cults) AB15	27	G3
Craig Pl. AB11	24	C4
Menzies Rd.		
Craig Pl. (Newt.), Stone. AB39	41	E4
Craigendarroch Av. AB16	13	F5
Craigendarroch Pl. AB16	13	F5
Craighaar Gables (Bucks.) AB21	8	C5
Stoneywood Rd.		
Craighead Av. (Port.) AB12	38	C3
Craighill Caravan Pk. (Bridge of Dee) AB12	30	A5
Craighill Ter. (Co.Bay) AB12	37	G1
Spark Ter.		
Craigie Loanings AB25	4	A2
Craigie Pk. AB25	4	A2
Craigie Pk. Pl. AB25	4	A2
Craigie St. AB25	4	C1
Craigiebuckler Av. AB15	22	C4
Craigiebuckler Dr. AB15	22	C4
Craigiebuckler Pl. AB15	22	C4
Craigiebuckler Ter. AB15	22	C4
Craigieburn Pk. AB15	22	D5
Craigielea Av. AB15	23	E5
Craigielea Gdns. AB15	23	E5
Craigielea Ms. AB15	23	E5
Craigievar Ct. AB10	29	G2
Craigievar Cres. AB10	29	F2
Craigievar Gdns. AB10	29	F2

Craigievar Pl. AB10	29	F1
Craigievar Rd. AB10	29	G2
Craigievar Ter. AB10	29	G2
Craigmarn Rd. (Port.) AB12	39	F4
Craigmaroinn Gdns. AB12	30	D5
Craignook Rd. (Dyce) AB21	7	G2
Balloch Way		
Craigpark AB12	30	D2
Craigshaw Cres. AB12	30	C1
Craigshaw Dr. AB12	30	C2
Craigshaw Pl. AB12	30	C1
Craigshaw Rd. AB12	30	C1
Craigshaw St. AB12	30	C1
Craigston Gdns., Westh. AB32	17	F3
Craigston Pl., Westh. AB32	17	F3
Craigston Rd., Westh. AB32	17	F3
Craigton Av. AB15	23	E6
Craigton Ct. AB15	23	F6
Craigton Cres., Peter. AB14	32	D3
Craigton Dr., Peter. AB14	32	D3
Craigton Gro., Peter. AB14	32	D3
Craigton Pk. AB15	23	E6
Craigton Rd. AB15	23	E6
Craigton Ter. AB15	23	E6
Craigton Ter., Peter. AB14	32	D3
Cranford Pl. AB10	23	F6
Cranford Rd. AB10	23	F6
Cranford Ter. AB10	23	F6
Cranhill Brae (Newt.), Stone. AB39	41	E4
Cranhill Pl. (Newt.), Stone. AB39	41	E3
Crathie Gdns. W. AB10	24	A6
Crathie Ter. AB10	23	H6
Crawpeel Rd. (Altens Ind. Est.) AB12	30	D4
Crawton Ness AB12	30	D5
Creel Av. (Co. Bay) AB12	37	E2
Creel Ct. (Co. Bay) AB12	37	E2
Creel Dr. (Co. Bay) AB12	37	F1
Creel Gdns. (Co. Bay) AB12	37	F1
Creel Pl. (Co. Bay) AB12	37	F2
Creel Rd. (Co. Bay) AB12	37	E2
Creel Wk. (Co. Bay) AB12	37	F1
Creel Wynd (Co. Bay) AB12	37	F2
Crimon Pl. AB10	4	C2
Croft Pl. AB16	22	C1
Croft Rd. AB16	22	C1
Croft Ter. AB16	13	E6
Crollshillock Pl. (Newt.), Stone. AB39	40	D4
Cromar Gdns. (Kings.) AB15	18	D4
Crombie Acres, Westh. AB32	16	B4
Crombie Circle, Peter. AB14	32	C2
Crombie Circle, Westh. AB32	16	C4
Crombie Cl., Westh. AB32	16	C4
Crombie Dr., Westh. AB32	16	B4
Crombie Pl. AB11	24	D4
Crombie Pl., Westh. AB32	16	B4
Crombie Acres		
Crombie Rd. AB11	24	D4
Crombie Rd., Westh. AB32	16	B4
Crombie Wynd, Westh. AB32	16	B4
Cromwell Ct. AB15	23	G4
Forbesfield Rd.		
Cromwell Gdns. AB15	23	F4
Cromwell Rd. AB15	23	F4
Crooked La. AB25	5	C1
Crookfold Gdns. (Br.Don) AB23	11	E6
Crookfold Pl. (Br.Don) AB23	11	E6
Crossgates (Bucks.) AB21	8	C6
Crown Cres., Peter. AB14	33	E2
Crown La. AB11	24	B3
Crown Ter.		
Crown Pl., Peter. AB14	33	E2
Crown St. AB11	5	C3
Crown Ter. AB11	5	C3
Crown Ter., Peter. AB14	33	E3
Cruden Cres. AB16	12	D4
Cruden Pk. AB16	12	D4
Cruden Pl. AB16	12	D4
Cruickshank Ct., Westh. AB32	16	B5
Cruickshank Cres. AB12	30	A3
Cruickshank Cres. (Bucks.) AB21	12	B2
Culter Den, Peter. AB14	32	C3
Culter Ho. Rd., Mill. AB13	26	A5
Cults Av. (Cults) AB15	27	H2
Cults Business Pk. (Cults) AB15	28	B2
Station Rd.		
Cults Ct. (Cults) AB15	28	A3
Cults Gdns. (Cults) AB15	28	A2
Cummings Pk. Circle AB16	13	G4
Cummings Pk. Cres. AB16	13	F4
Cummings Pk. Dr. AB16	13	F4
Cummings Pk. Rd. AB16	13	G3
Cummings Pk. Ter. AB16	13	F4
Cuparstone Ct. AB10	24	A3
Cuparstone Row		
Cuparstone La. AB10	24	A3
Cuparstone Row		
Cuparstone Row AB10	4	B3
Cypress Av. (Br.Don) AB23	10	D2
Cypress Gro. (Br.Don) AB23	10	D2
Cypress Wk. (Br.Don) AB23	10	D2

D

Dalmaik Cres., Peter. AB14	32	D2
Dalmaik Ter., Peter. AB14	32	D2
Dalmuinzie Rd. (Bield.) AB15	27	E3
Dancing Cairns Cres. AB16	13	E3
Dancing Cairns Pl. AB16	13	E2
Danestone Pl. (Br.Don) AB23	15	E1
Danestone Ter. (Br.Don) AB23	15	E1
Darroch Pk. (Cults) AB15	27	H3
Davan Pk. (Br.Don) AB22	14	D1
Davidson Dr. AB16	12	D3
Davidson Gdns. AB16	12	D4
Davidson Ho. AB15	22	B3
Hazlehead Rd.		
Davidson Pl. AB16	12	D4
Dawson Brae, Westh. AB32	16	B4
Dawson Cl., Westh. AB32	16	B4
Dawson Dr., Westh. AB32	16	B4
Dawson Way, Westh. AB32	16	B3
Dawson Wynd, Westh. AB32	16	B4
Dean Gdns., Westh. AB32	17	F4
Deansloch Cres. AB16	13	E4
Deansloch Pl. AB16	13	E4
Deansloch Ter. AB16	13	E4
Dee Pl. AB11	5	C3
Dee St. AB11	4	C3
Deemount Av. AB11	24	B5
Deemount Gdns. AB11	24	B5
Deemount Rd. AB11	24	B5
Deemount Ter. AB11	24	B5
Deer Rd. (Woodside) AB24	14	A3
Deeside Av. AB15	29	E1
Deeside Cres. AB15	29	E1
Deeside Dr. AB15	29	E1
Deeside Gdns. AB15	29	E1
Deeside Pk. AB15	29	E1
Deeside Pl. AB15	29	E1
Deeside Ter. AB15	29	E1
Deevale Cres. AB12	30	A2
Deevale Gdns. AB12	30	A2
Deevale Rd. AB12	30	A2
Deevale Ter. AB12	30	A2
Deeview Rd. S. (Cults) AB15	28	A3
Delgaty La. (Dyce) AB21	7	F2
Belmuir Gdns.		
Dempsey Ter. AB24	14	C3
Den, The (Cults) AB15	28	B3
Den of Cults (Cults) AB15	28	B2
Denburn Ct. AB25	24	B1
Gilcomston Pk.		
Denburn Rd. AB11	4	C2
Denburn Rd. AB11	4	C2
Denmore Ct. (Br.Don) AB23	11	E3
Dubford Rd.		
Denmore Gdns. (Br.Don) AB22	14	D1
Denmore Ind. Est. (Br.Don) AB23	11	E3
Denmore Pl. (Br.Don) AB23	11	E3
Denmore Rd. (Br.Don) AB23	11	E3
Denseat Ct. AB15	22	A2
Queens Den		
Denseat Rd. AB15	22	A2
Denwood AB15	22	B2
Derbeth Cres. AB16	22	A1
Derbeth Pk. (Kings.) AB15	18	D2
Derbeth Pl. (Kings.) AB15	18	D2
Derry Av. AB16	13	F6
Derry Pl. AB16	13	F6
Desswood Pl. AB15	23	G3
Desswood Pl. AB25	23	G3
Devanha Cres. AB11	24	B4
Devanha Gdns. AB11	24	B4
Devanha Gdns. E. AB11	24	B4
Devanha Gdns. S. AB11	24	B5
Devanha Gdns. W. AB11	24	B4
Devanha La. AB11	24	B4
Devanha Gdns.		
Devanha Ter. AB11	24	B4
Devenick Dr. (Port.) AB12	39	E2
Devenick Pl. AB10	29	F2
Deveron Rd. AB16	12	D5
Devonshire Rd. AB10	23	G4
Diamond La. AB10	24	B2
Diamond St.		
Diamond Pl. AB10	24	B2
Union Ter.		
Diamond St. AB10	4	C2
Dickson Ter. AB10	12	D5
Dill Pl. AB24	14	B2
Dill Rd. AB24	14	B2
Dinbaith Pl. AB16	22	A1
Derbeth Cres.		
Dock St. E. AB11	25	E3
Blaikies Quay		
Dock St. W. AB11	25	E3
Blaikies Quay		
Dominies Ct. AB16	13	H4
Dominies Rd. AB16	13	H4
Don Ct. (Woodside) AB24	13	H2
Don Gdns. (Woodside) AB24	14	A2
Don Pl. (Dyce) AB21	7	F3
Don Pl. AB24	14	B3
Don St. (Old Aberdeen) AB24	14	D3
Don St. (Woodside) AB24	14	B3
Don Ter. (Woodside) AB24	14	A2
Donald Pl. AB25	4	B1
Donbank Ter. AB24	14	B2
Donmouth Ct. (Br.Don) AB23	15	F1
Donmouth Cres. (Br.Don) AB23	15	F1
Donmouth Gdns. (Br.Don) AB23	15	F1
Donmouth Rd. (Br.Don) AB23	15	F2
Donmouth Ter. (Br.Don) AB23	15	F1
Donside Ct. AB24	14	B2
Auchinleck Rd.		
Donview Ho. AB24	15	F3
Donview Pl. AB24	14	B2
Donview Rd. AB24	14	A2
Doolie Ness AB12	30	D5
Douglas La. AB24	14	D4
High St.		
Douglas Pl. AB24	14	D4
High St.		
Downies Brae AB11	24	D5
Downies Pl. AB11	25	E5
Downies Rd. (Port.) AB12	39	E4
Drinnies Cres. (Dyce) AB21	7	G2
Drumthwacket Dr. (Port.) AB12	38	C5
Dubford Av. (Br.Don) AB23	10	D3
Dubford Cres. (Br.Don) AB23	10	D3
Dubford Gdns. (Br.Don) AB23	10	D2
Dubford Gro. (Br.Don) AB23	10	D2
Dubford Pk. (Br.Don) AB23	10	D4
Dubford Pl. (Br.Don) AB23	10	D3
Dubford Ri. (Br.Don) AB23	10	D2
Dubford Rd. (Br.Don) AB23	10	D3
Dubford Ter. (Br.Don) AB23	10	D3
Dubford Wk. (Br.Don) AB23	10	D2
Duff St. AB24	5	E1
Dugald Baird Ct. AB12	30	A4
Clerk Maxwell Cres.		
Dugald Baird Sq. AB12	30	A4
Clerk Maxwell Cres.		
Dulnain Rd. AB16	12	D6
Dumgoyne Pl. AB15	22	D2
Dunbar St. AB24	14	D4
Dunbennan Rd. (Dyce) AB21	7	G2
Duncans Pl. AB24	14	D4
High St.		
Dunecht Gdns., Westh. AB32	16	C4
Dunecht Rd., Westh. AB32	16	C4
Dunlin Ct. (Newt.), Stone. AB39	41	E3
Dunlin Cres. (Co.Bay) AB12	30	D6
Dunlin Rd. (Co.Bay) AB12	30	C6
Dunmail Av. (Cults) AB15	28	A3
Dunnyfell Rd. (Muchalls), Stone. AB39	40	B6
Dunvegan Av. (Port.) AB12	38	D3
Dunvegan Cres. (Port.) AB12	38	D3
Dunvegan Pl. (Port.) AB12	38	D3
Duthie Ct. AB10	23	F5
Duthie Ter.		
Duthie Pl. AB10	23	F6

Name	Page	Grid
Duthie Ter. AB10	23	F6
Dyce Dr. (Dyce) AB21	6	D6
Dyce Ind. Est. (Dyce) AB21	7	G6
Dyce Shopping Cen. (Dyce) AB21	7	H3
Dykeside Way (Bucks.) AB21	12	B3
Newhills Av.		
E		
Earls Ct. Gdns. AB15	23	E3
Earlspark Av. (Bield.) AB15	27	F2
Earlspark Circle (Bield.) AB15	27	F2
Earlspark Cres. (Bield.) AB15	27	F2
Earlspark Dr. (Bield.) AB15	27	F3
Earlspark Gdns. (Bield.) AB15	27	F2
Earlspark Pl. (Bield.) AB15	27	F3
Earlspark Way (Bield.) AB15	27	G2
Earlspark Av.		
Earlswells Dr. (Cults) AB15	27	G3
Earlswells Pl. (Cults) AB15	27	G3
Earlswells Rd. (Cults) AB15	27	G3
Earlswells Vw. (Cults) AB15	27	G2
Earlswells Wk. (Cults) AB15	27	G3
Earn's Heugh Av. (Co.Bay) AB12	37	F1
Earn's Heugh Circle (Co.Bay) AB12	37	F1
Earn's Heugh Cres. (Co.Bay) AB12	37	F1
Earn's Heugh Pl. (Co.Bay) AB12	30	D6
Earn's Heugh Rd. AB12	30	D5
Earn's Heugh Vw. (Co.Bay) AB12	30	D6
Earn's Heugh Wk. (Co.Bay) AB12	30	D6
Earn's Heugh Way (Co.Bay) AB12	37	F1
Earnsheugh Rd. (Port.) AB12	39	H2
Earnsheugh Ter. (Port.) AB12	39	H2
East Craibstone St. AB11	24	B4
Bon Accord St.		
East Grn. AB11	24	C2
Market St.		
East Main Av. AB16	13	F6
East N. St. AB24	5	D1
East Tullos Ind. Est. AB12	25	E6
Easter Ct. (Port.) AB12	38	D5
Easter Dr. (Port.) AB12	38	D5
Easter Pl. (Port.) AB12	38	D5
Eastside Av., Westh. AB32	17	E4
Eastside Dr., Westh. AB32	17	E3
Eastside Grn., Westh. AB32	17	E3
Eastsyde Pl. (Port.) AB12	38	C5
Eday Cres. AB15	22	B1
Eday Dr. AB15	22	B1
Eday Gdns. AB15	22	A2
Eday Rd. AB15	22	C2
Eday Sq. AB15	22	B1
Eday Wk. AB15	22	B2
Eden Pl. AB25	4	B1
Edgehill Rd. AB15	23	E2
Edgehill Ter. AB15	23	E2
Edmond Gdns. (Kings.) AB15	18	D5
Eidenside, Peter. AB14	32	C2
Elder Pl. AB25	14	A5
Ellerslie Rd. (Bucks.) AB21	8	C6
Ellon Rd. (Br.Don) AB23	11	F6
Elm Pl. AB25	14	B6
Elmbank Rd. AB24	14	D6
Elmbank Ter. AB24	14	C5
Elmfield Av. AB24	14	C5
Elmfield Pl. AB24	14	C5
Elmfield Ter. AB24	14	C5
Elphinstone Ct. AB24	14	B2
Auchinleck Cres.		
Elphinstone Rd. AB24	14	D4
Elrick Circle (Br.Don) AB22	10	C6
Elsick Pl. (Newt.), Stone. AB39	40	D4
Endrick Pl. AB15	22	D1
Enterprise Dr., Westh. AB32	16	D6
Eriskay Dr. AB16	21	H1
Errol Pl. AB24	15	E6
Errol St. AB24	15	E6
Erskine St. AB24	14	C5
Esk Pl. AB16	13	E5
Esplanade AB24	25	E2
Esslemont Av. AB25	4	A1
Exchange La. AB11	24	C2
Exchange St.		
Exchange St. AB11	5	D2
Exchequer Row AB11	24	C2
Shiprow		
Exhibition Av. (Br.Don) AB23	11	F6
Exploration Dr. (Br.Don) AB23	11	F5
F		
Fairies Knowe (Bucks.) AB21	12	B2
Fairley Den (Bucks.) AB21	12	B1
Sclattie Pk.		
Fairley Rd. (Kings.) AB15	18	D5
Fairlie St. AB16	13	G3
Fairview Av. (Dane.) AB22	9	H6
Fairview Brae (Dane.) AB22	13	H1
Fairview Circle (Dane.) AB22	9	G6
Fairview Cres. (Dane.) AB22	9	H6
Fairview Dr. (Dane.) AB22	13	H1
Fairview Gdns. (Dane.) AB22	9	G6
Fairview Gra. (Br.Don) AB22	9	G6
Fairview Gro. (Dane.) AB22	9	H6
Fairview Manor (Dane.) AB22	13	H1
Fairview Par. (Dane.) AB22	9	H6
Fairview Pk. (Dane.) AB22	9	H6
Fairview Pl. (Dane.) AB22	9	H6
Fairview Rd. (Dane.) AB22	9	G6
Fairview St. (Dane.) AB22	9	H6
Fairview Ter. (Dane.) AB22	9	G6
Fairview Wk. (Dane.) AB22	10	A6
Fairview Way (Dane.) AB22	9	H6
Fairview Wynd (Dane.) AB22	10	A6
Falkland Av. (Co.Bay) AB12	31	E6
Fallow Pl., Westh. AB32	16	B4
Fara Cl. AB15	21	H1
Farburn Ind. Est. (Dyce) AB21	7	G5
Farburn Ter. (Dyce) AB21	7	F4
Fare Pk. Circle, Westh. AB32	16	D3
Fare Pk. Cres., Westh. AB32	17	E3
Fare Pk. Dr., Westh. AB32	16	D4
Fare Pk. Gdns., Westh. AB32	16	D4
Farmers Hall La. AB25	4	B1
Farquhar Av. AB11	25	E5
Farquhar Brae AB11	25	E5
Farquhar Rd. AB11	24	D6
Farrier La. AB24	24	C1
Mealmarket St.		
Fassiefern Av. (Br.Don) AB23	11	E4
Faulds Cres. AB12	30	A1
Faulds Gate AB12	30	A2
Faulds Row AB12	30	B2
Faulds Wynd AB12	30	B1
Fergus Pl. (Dyce) AB21	7	F2
Ferguson St. (Bucks.) AB21	12	D1
Oldmeldrum Rd.		
Fern Dr. (Port.) AB12	38	D4
Fern Pl. (Port.) AB12	38	D4
Fernhill Dr. AB16	13	E6
Fernhill Pl. AB16	22	B1
Fernhill Rd. AB16	22	B1
Fernie Brae AB11	24	D6
Fernielea Cres. AB15	22	C2
Fernielea Pl. AB15	22	C2
Fernielea Rd. AB15	22	C2
Ferrier Cres. AB24	14	B3
Ferrier Gdns. AB24	14	B3
Ferry Pl. AB11	25	E3
Ferryhill Gdns. AB11	24	B4
Ferryhill La. AB11	24	B4
Ferryhill Pl. AB11	24	B4
Ferryhill Rd. AB11	24	B4
Ferryhill Ter. AB11	24	B4
Fetach Wk. (Dyce) AB21	7	F2
Fifehill Pk. AB21	7	G3
Findhorn Pl. AB16	12	D6
Findon Ness AB12	31	E5
Findon Pl. (Port.) AB12	39	H1
Findon Rd. (Port.) AB12	39	G1
Finnan Brae AB11	25	F4
Finnan Pl. AB11	25	F4
Finnan Brae		
Fintray Rd. AB15	22	C4
Firhill Pl. AB24	14	D5
Spital Wk.		
Firhill Rd. AB24	14	D5
Fish St. AB11	5	E2
Fittick Pl. (Co.Bay) AB12	31	E6
Flourmill La. AB10	5	D2
Fonthill Gdns. E. AB11	24	A4
Fonthill Gdns. W. AB11	24	A4
Fonthill Rd. AB11	24	A4
Fonthill Ter. AB11	24	A4
Forbes St. AB25	4	B1
Forbesfield La. AB15	23	G4
Forbesfield Rd. AB15	23	G4
Forehill La. (Br.Don) AB22	10	D6
Glashieburn Way		
Forest Av. AB15	23	G4
Forest Av. La. AB15	23	G4
Forest Rd. AB15	23	F2
Foresterhill Ct. AB25	23	G1
Foresters Av. (Bucks.) AB21	8	C5
Forestgait AB15	23	F2
Formartine Rd. AB24	14	B3
Forresterhill Rd. AB16	13	G5
Forresterhill Rd. AB25	13	H6
Forrit Brae (Bucks.) AB21	8	A6
Forties Rd. (Dyce) AB21	6	C4
Forvie Av. (Br.Don) AB22	10	C5
Forvie Circle (Br.Don) AB22	10	C4
Forvie Cl. (Br.Don) AB22	10	C4
Forvie Cres. (Br.Don) AB22	10	C5
Forvie La. (Br.Don) AB22	10	C5
Forvie Pk. AB22	10	C5
Jesmond Rd.		
Forvie Path (Br.Don) AB22	10	C5
Forvie Pl. (Br.Don) AB22	10	C5
Forvie Rd. (Br.Don) AB22	10	C4
Forvie St. (Br.Don) AB22	10	C4
Forvie Ter. (Br.Don) AB22	10	C5
Forvie Way (Br.Don) AB22	10	C5
Fountainhall Rd. AB15	23	G2
Fountville Ct. AB24	14	A3
Summer St.		
Foveran Path (Br.Don) AB22	10	C5
Foveran Ri. (Br.Don) AB22	10	B4
Foveran St. (Br.Don) AB22	10	B4
Foveran Way (Br.Don) AB22	10	B5
Fowler Av. AB16	13	F3
Fowlershill Gdns. (Br.Don) AB22	14	D1
Fraser Ct. AB25	14	D6
Fraser Dr., Westh. AB32	16	C5
Fraser Pl. AB25	14	C6
Fraser Rd. AB25	14	C6
Fraser St. AB25	14	C6
Fraserfield Gdns. (Br.Don) AB23	15	E1
Frederick St. AB24	5	D1
Friarsfield Rd. (Cults) AB15	28	A2
Friendship Ter. AB10	23	H4
Ashley Rd.		
Froghall Av. AB24	14	D6
Froghall Gdns. AB24	14	D6
Froghall Pl. AB24	14	D5
Froghall Rd. AB24	14	D6
Froghall Ter. AB24	14	D6
Froghall Vw. AB24	14	D5
Fullerton Ct. AB24	13	G2
Fulmar Ct. (Newt.), Stone. AB39	41	E3
G		
Gadie Cres. AB16	13	E5
Gaelic La. AB10	24	B2
Belmont St.		
Gairn Circle AB10	24	A5
Gairn Ct. AB10	24	A5
Gairn Cres. AB10	24	A5
Gairn Rd. AB10	24	A5
Gairn Ter. AB10	24	A5
Gairnshiel Av. AB16	13	F5
Gairnshiel Pl. AB16	13	F5
Gairsay Dr. AB15	22	B1
Gairsay Rd. AB15	22	B1
Gairsay Sq. AB15	22	B1
Gaitside Cres. AB10	29	E2
Gaitside Dr. AB10	29	E2
Gaitside Pl. AB10	29	F1
Gaitside Rd. AB10	29	E2
Gaitside Ter. AB10	29	E2
Gallowgate AB10	5	D1
Gallowgate AB25	5	D1
Gallowhill Ter. (Dyce) AB21	7	H2
Garden City AB15	22	D1
Garden Ct. AB23	11	E4
Garden Rd. (Cults) AB15	27	H2
Gardner Cres. AB12	29	H3
Gardner Dr. AB12	29	H3
Gardner Pl. AB12	29	H3
Gardner Rd. AB12	29	H2
Gardner Wk. AB12	30	A3
Garmaddie La. (Dyce) AB21	7	F2
Sluie Dr.		
Garthdee Cres. AB10	29	G1

Name	Page	Grid
Garthdee Dr. AB10	29	G1
Garthdee Gdns. AB10	29	G1
Garthdee Rd. AB10	29	G2
Garthdee Rd. (Cults) AB15	29	F2
Garthdee Ter. AB10	29	G1
Garvock Wynd AB11	5	E2
George St. AB25	14	D4
Gerrard St. AB25	5	C1
Gilbert Rd. (Bucks.) AB21	12	C1
Gilcomston Ct. AB10	24	A2
Kidd St.		
Gilcomston Land AB10	24	A2
Kidd St.		
Gilcomston Pk. AB25	4	B2
Gilcomston Steps AB25	4	B1
Gilcomston Ter. AB25	24	A1
Farmers Hall La.		
Gillahill Pl. AB16	13	F6
Gillahill Rd. AB16	13	F6
Gillespie Cres. AB25	14	A5
Gillespie Pl. AB25	14	A5
Girdleness Rd. AB11	25	E5
Girdleness Ter. AB11	24	D6
Girdlestone Pl. AB11	25	E5
Gladstone Pl. AB10	23	G3
Gladstone Pl. (Dyce) AB21	7	F3
Gladstone Pl. (Woodside) AB24	14	A2
Glascairn Av. (Port.) AB12	38	D3
Glascairn Pl. (Port.) AB12	38	D3
Glashieburn Av. (Br.Don) AB22	10	C4
Glashieburn Way (Br.Don) AB22	10	D6
Glebe Ct. (Port.) AB12	39	E3
Glen Av. (Dyce) AB21	7	F3
Glen Dr. (Dyce) AB21	7	F3
Glen Gdns. (Dyce) AB21	7	F3
Glen Rd. (Dyce) AB21	7	F3
Glenbervie Rd. AB11	24	D4
Glendale Ms. AB11	24	A3
Union Glen		
Glendee Ter. (Cults) AB15	28	B2
Gleneagles Av. (Br.Don) AB22	10	C5
Gleneagles Dr. (Br.Don) AB22	10	C5
Gleneagles Gdns. (Br.Don) AB22	10	C5
Gleneagles Wk. (Br.Don) AB22	10	C5
Gleneagles Av.		
Glenhome Av. (Dyce) AB21	7	F4
Glenhome Ct. (Dyce) AB21	7	G3
Glenhome Cres. (Dyce) AB21	7	F4
Glenhome Gdns. (Dyce) AB21	7	F4
Glenhome Ter. (Dyce) AB21	7	F4
Glenhome Wk. (Dyce) AB21	7	G4
Glentanar Cres. (Dyce) AB21	7	G2
Golden Sq. AB10	4	C2
Golf Rd. (Bield.) AB15	27	G4
Golf Rd. AB24	15	F5
Golfview Rd. (Bield.) AB15	27	G4
Goodhope Rd. (Bucks.) AB21	13	E1
Gordon Av. (Br.Don) AB23	11	E6
Gordon Barracks (Br.Don) AB23	11	F6
Gordon Cl., Westh. AB32	16	D4
Gordon Gdns., Westh. AB32	17	E4
Gordon La. AB15	23	E6
Gordon Lennox Cres. AB23	11	E4
Gordon Rd. AB15	23	E6
Gordon Rd. (Br.Don) AB23	11	E6
Gordon St. AB11	4	C3
Gordon Ter. AB15	23	E6
Gordon Ter. (Dyce) AB21	7	F3
Gordondale Ct. AB15	23	F2
Gordondale Rd. AB15	23	G1
Gordon's Mills Cres. AB24	14	B2
Gordon's Mills Pl. AB24	14	B2
Gordon's Mills Rd. AB24	14	A2
Gorse Circle (Port.) AB12	38	C5
Gort Rd. AB24	14	B2
Gort Ter. AB24	14	B2
Auchinleck Rd.		
Goval Ter. (Dyce) AB21	7	G3
Gowanbrae Rd. (Bield.) AB15	27	F4
Graeme Av. (Dyce) AB21	7	F3
Grampian Ct. AB11	25	F5
Balnagask Circle		
Grampian Gdns. (Dyce) AB21	7	H4
Grampian La. AB11	24	D4
Grampian Pl. AB11	24	C5
Grampian Rd. AB11	24	D5
Grandholm Br. (Private) AB22	14	A2
Grandholm Ct. AB24	14	B2
Montgomery Rd.		
Grandholm St. AB24	14	A3
Grange, The, Westh. AB32	16	C4
Granitehill Pl. AB16	13	G5
Granitehill Rd. AB16	13	F3
Granitehill Ter. (Persley) AB22	13	F1
Grant Cl., Westh. AB32	17	E4
Granton Pl. AB10	4	A3
Grants Pl. AB24	14	D4
High St.		
Granville Pl. AB10	23	G5
Gray Ct. AB15	22	C2
Gray St. AB10	23	G5
Gray St. Ms. AB10	23	G5
Great Northern Rd. AB24	13	G2
Great Southern Rd. AB10	24	A5
Great Southern Rd. AB11	24	A5
Great Southern Rd. AB12	30	A1
Great Western Pl. AB10	23	H4
Great Western Rd. AB10	23	F5
Green, The AB11	24	C2
Rennies Wynd		
Green, The (Port.) AB12	38	D4
Greenbank Cres. AB12	30	D1
Greenbank Pl. AB12	30	D1
Greenbank Rd. AB12	30	D1
Greenbrae Av. (Br.Don) AB23	11	E4
Greenbrae Circle (Br.Don) AB23	11	E3
Greenbrae Cres. (Br.Don) AB23	11	E3
Greenbrae Dr. (Br.Don) AB23	11	E3
Greenbrae Gdns. N. AB23	11	E3
Greenbrae Gdns. S. AB23	11	E3
Greenbrae Wk. (Br.Don) AB23	11	E3
Greenburn Dr. (Bucks.) AB21	8	B6
Greenburn Pk. (Bucks.) AB21	8	B6
Greenburn Rd. (Bucks.) AB21	8	C6
Greenburn Rd. N. AB21	8	A5
Greenburn Ter. (Bucks.) AB21	12	B1
Greenfern Av. AB16	12	D6
Greenfern Pl. AB16	12	D6
Greenfern Rd.		
Greenfern Rd. AB16	12	D6
Greenhole Pl. AB23	10	D5
Greenmore Gdns. AB24	14	B4
Greenwell Pl. AB12	25	E6
Greenwell Rd. AB12	25	E6
Gregness Gdns. AB11	25	E6
Greig Ct. AB25	5	C1
Greyhope Rd. AB11	25	G3
Greystone Pl. (Newt.), Stone. AB39	41	E4
Groats Rd. AB15	22	A3
Grosvenor Pl. AB25	4	A2
Grosvenor Ter. AB25	24	A2
Grosvenor Pl.		
Grove Cres. AB16	14	A6
Guestrow AB10	24	C2
Broad St.		
Guild St. AB11	5	D3
Gullymoss Gdns., Westh. AB32	17	E3
Gullymoss Pl., Westh. AB32	17	E3
Gullymoss Vw., Westh. AB32	17	E3
H		
Hadden St. AB11	24	C2
Market St.		
Hallfield Cres. AB16	22	B1
Hallfield Rd. AB16	22	B1
Hamilton La. AB15	23	F2
Hamilton Pl.		
Hamilton Pl. AB15	23	F2
Hammerfield Av. AB10	23	F5
Hammersmith Rd. AB10	23	G5
Hanover St. AB11	5	E1
Harcourt Rd. AB15	23	F1
Hardgate AB10	24	A5
Hardgate AB11	24	A4
Hardgate La. AB10	24	A5
Hardgate		
Harehill Rd. (Br.Don) AB22	10	C6
Hareness Circle AB12	31	E3
Hareness Pk. AB12	31	E3
Hareness Rd. AB12	30	D3
Harlaw Pl. AB15	23	F4
Harlaw Rd. AB15	23	F4
Harlaw Ter. AB15	23	F4
Harley Ter. (Port.) AB12	39	G4
Harriet St. AB25	5	C2
Harris Dr. AB24	14	C3
Harrow Rd. AB24	15	E3
Harthill Pl. AB16	12	C6
Hartington Rd. AB10	23	G3
Harvest Hill, Westh. AB32	16	B4
Hasman Ter. (Co.Bay) AB12	37	G1
Spark Ter.		
Hawthorn Cres. AB16	13	F5
Hawthorn Ter. AB24	15	F6
Urquhart Pl.		
Hayfield Cres. AB24	14	A5
Hayfield Pl. AB24	14	A4
Hays Way, Westh. AB32	16	D4
Hayton Rd. AB24	14	B3
Hazel Dr., Westh. AB32	16	D5
Hazledene AB15	22	B3
Hazledene Rd. AB15	22	C4
Hazlehead Av. AB15	22	B3
Hazlehead Caravan Pk. AB15	22	A3
Hazlehead Cres. AB15	22	B3
Hazlehead Gdns. AB15	22	A3
Hazlehead Pl. AB15	22	B3
Hazlehead Rd. AB15	22	B3
Hazlehead Ter. AB15	22	A3
Headland Ct. AB10	29	H1
Headland Ct. (Newt.), Stone. AB39	41	E4
Villagelands Rd.		
Heather Pl. (Port.) AB12	38	D3
Heathfield Pk. (Newt.), Stone. AB39	40	D4
Heathryfold Circle AB16	13	E3
Heathryfold Dr. AB16	13	E3
Heathryfold Pl. AB16	13	E3
Henderson Dr., Westh. AB32	16	D5
Hermitage Av. AB24	14	D4
Hetherwick Rd. AB12	29	H3
High St. AB24	14	D4
Highgate Gdns. AB11	24	B5
Hill of Rubislaw AB15	22	D4
Hill St. AB25	4	B1
Hill Vw. Gdns. AB12	24	D6
Hill Vw. Pl. AB12	30	D1
Hillcrest Pl. AB16	13	G4
Cummings Pk. Circle		
Hillhead Rd. (Bield.) AB15	26	D3
Hillhead Rd. (Newt.), Stone. AB39	41	E4
Hillhead Ter. AB24	14	D5
Spital		
Hillocks Way (Bucks.) AB21	12	C2
Hillside Cres., Peter. AB14	32	D2
Hillside Cres., Westh. AB32	17	E3
Hillside Gdns., Westh. AB32	17	E3
Hillside Pl., Peter. AB14	32	D2
Hillside Rd., Peter. AB14	32	D3
Hillside Rd., Westh. AB32	17	E3
Hillside Ter. (Port.) AB12	39	E3
Hillside Vw., Westh. AB32	17	E3
Hillswick Rd. AB16	12	B6
Hillswick Wk. AB16	12	B6
Hilltop Av. (Cults) AB15	27	H2
Hilltop Av., Westh. AB32	16	D3
Hilltop Cres., Westh. AB32	16	D3
Hilltop Dr., Westh. AB32	16	D3
Hilltop Gdns., Westh. AB32	17	E3
Hilltop Rd. (Cults) AB15	27	H2
Hillview Av., Westh. AB32	17	E3
Hillview Cres. (Cults) AB15	27	G2
Hillview Dr. (Cults) AB15	27	H2
Hillview Rd. AB12	24	D6
Hillview Rd. (Cults) AB15	27	H3
Hillview Rd., Peter. AB14	32	D3
Hillview Rd., Westh. AB32	17	E3
Hillview Ter. (Cults) AB15	27	H3
Hillylands Rd. AB16	22	C1
Hilton Av. AB24	13	H4
Hilton Circle AB24	14	A5
Hilton Ct. AB24	13	H4
Hilton Dr. AB24	14	A4
Hilton Pl. AB24	14	B4
Hilton Rd. AB24	13	H4
Hilton St. AB24	14	A5
Hilton Ter. AB24	14	A4
Hilton Wk. AB24	14	A4
Holburn Pl. AB10	23	H5
Holburn Rd. AB10	23	H4
Holburn St. AB10	24	A5
Holland Pl. AB25	14	C6
Holland St. AB25	14	C6

Street	Page	Grid
Hollybank Pl. AB11	24	A4
Holmhead Pl. (Bucks.) AB21	12	B2
Newhills Av.		
Homelea, Westh. AB32	16	B5
Hopecroft Av. (Bucks.) AB21	8	B6
Hopecroft Dr. (Bucks.) AB21	8	B6
Hopecroft Gdns. (Bucks.) AB21	12	B1
Hopecroft Ter. (Bucks.) AB21	8	B6
Hopetoun Av. (Bucks.) AB21	12	A1
Hopetoun Ct. (Bucks.) AB21	12	B1
Hopetoun Cres. (Bucks.) AB21	12	A1
Hopetoun Dr. (Bucks.) AB21	12	A1
Hopetoun Gra. (Bucks.) AB21	12	A1
Hopetoun Grn. (Bucks.) AB21	12	B1
Hopetoun Rd. (Bucks.) AB21	12	A1
Hopetoun Ter. (Bucks.) AB21	12	A1
Hosefield Av. AB15	23	G1
Hosefield Rd. AB15	23	G1
Howburn Pl. AB11	24	A4
Howe Moss Av. AB21	6	B3
Howe Moss Cres. AB21	6	B3
Howe Moss Dr. AB21	6	B4
Howe Moss Pl. AB21	6	B3
Howe Moss Rd. AB21	6	B3
Howe Moss Ter. AB21	6	C2
Howes Cres. AB16	12	D3
Howes Dr. AB16	12	D3
Howes Pk. AB16	13	E3
Howes Cres.		
Howes Pl. AB16	12	D3
Howes Cres.		
Howes Rd. (Bucks.) AB21	12	C3
Howes Vw. (Bucks.) AB21	12	C2
Howie La., Peter. AB14	33	E4
Hunter Pl. AB24	15	E6
Huntly St. AB10	4	B2
Hutcheon Ct. AB25	14	D6
Hutcheon Gdns. (Br.Don) AB23	15	E1
Hutcheon Low Dr. AB21	13	F2
Hutcheon Low Pl. AB21	13	G2
Hutcheon St. AB25	4	B1
Hutchison Ter. AB10	23	F6
Hutton La. AB16	13	E4
Byron Cres.		
Hutton Pl. AB16	13	E4
Huxterstone Ct. (Kings.) AB15	18	D5
Huxterstone Dr. (Kings.) AB15	18	D5
Huxterstone Pl. (Kings.) AB15	18	C5
Huxterstone Ter. (Kings.) AB15	18	D5

I

Street	Page	Grid
Imperial Pl. AB11	24	C2
Guild St.		
Inchbrae Dr. AB10	29	E2
Inchbrae Rd. AB10	29	F2
Inchbrae Ter. AB10	29	E2
Inchgarth Rd. (Cults) AB15	28	C2
Ingram Wk. AB12	30	C3
Intown Rd. (Br.Don) AB23	11	F6
Invercauld Gdns. AB16	13	F5
Invercauld Pl. AB16	13	E5
Invercauld Rd.		
Invercauld Rd. AB16	13	E5
Inverdon Ct. AB24	15	E2
Inverurie Rd. (Bucks.) AB21	12	C1
Irvine Pl. AB10	23	H5
Isla Pl. AB16	12	D6
Ivanhoe Pl. AB10	29	E1
Ivanhoe Rd. AB10	29	E1
Ivanhoe Wk. AB10	29	E1

J

Street	Page	Grid
Jacks Brae AB25	4	B2
Jackson Ter. AB24	15	E6
Urquhart La.		
Jamaica St. AB25	14	C6
James St. AB11	5	E2
Jamiesons Quay AB11	5	D3
Jasmine Pl. AB24	5	D1
Jasmine Ter. AB24	5	D1
Jasmine Way AB24	5	D1
Jesmond Av. (Br.Don) AB22	10	C4
Jesmond Av. N. (Br.Don) AB22	10	A4
Jesmond Circle (Br.Don) AB22	10	A3
Jesmond Ct. (Br.Don) AB22	10	C4
Jesmond Dr. (Br.Don) AB22	10	A3
Jesmond Gdns. (Br.Don) AB22	10	A3
Jesmond Gro. (Br.Don) AB22	10	A3
Jesmond Rd. (Br.Don) AB22	10	B5
Jesmond Sq. (Br.Don) AB22	10	B5
Jesmond Sq. E. (Br.Don) AB22	10	B5
Jesmond Sq.		
Jesmond Sq. N. (Br.Don) AB22	10	B5
Jesmond Sq.		
Jesmond Sq. S. (Br.Don) AB22	10	B5
Jesmond Sq.		
John Arthur Ct. (Kings.) AB15	19	E6
John St. (Dyce) AB21	7	F4
John St. AB25	4	C1
Johns Pk. Pl. AB22	14	A1
Johnston Gdns. E., Peter. AB14	32	C2
Johnston Gdns. N., Peter. AB14	32	D2
Johnston Gdns. W., Peter. AB14	32	D2
Jopps La. AB25	5	C1
Jubilee Gait AB10	23	H6
Juniper Pl. (Port.) AB12	38	C4
Jura Pl. AB16	22	A1
Justice Mill Brae AB11	24	A3
Justice Mill La.		
Justice Mill La. AB11	4	B3
Justice Port AB24	24	D1
Beach Boul.		
Justice St. AB11	5	D2
Jute St. AB24	14	D6

K

Street	Page	Grid
Kaimhill Circle AB10	29	G1
Kaimhill Gdns. AB10	29	G1
Kaimhill Rd. AB10	29	F1
Keir Circle, Westh. AB32	16	C4
Kemnay Pl. AB15	22	C4
Kemp St. AB16	13	G3
Kenfield Cres. AB15	23	E5
Kenfield Pl. AB15	23	E5
Kennerty Ct., Peter. AB14	32	D4
Kennerty Mills Rd.		
Kennerty Mills Rd., Peter. AB14	32	D4
Kennerty Pk., Peter. AB14	32	D4
Kennerty Rd., Peter. AB14	32	C4
Kepplehills Dr. (Bucks.) AB21	12	B1
Kepplehills Rd. (Bucks.) AB21	12	B2
Kepplestone Av. AB15	23	E4
Kerloch Gdns. AB11	24	C5
Kerloch Pl. AB11	24	C6
Kettlehills Cres. AB16	13	F4
Kettlehills La. AB16	13	F4
Kettlehills Rd. AB16	13	E4
Kettock Gdns. (Br.Don) AB22	10	B5
Mundurno Rd.		
Kettocks Mill Rd. AB22	14	C2
Kidd St. AB10	4	B2
Kildrummy Rd. AB15	22	C4
Kilsyth Rd. AB12	30	C2
Kinaldie Cres. AB15	22	C4
Kincorth Circle AB12	30	A2
Kincorth Cres. AB12	30	B1
Kincorth Gdns. AB12	30	B1
Kincorth Land AB12	30	B2
Kincorth Pl. AB12	30	A1
King George VI Br. AB10	24	B6
King St. AB24	15	E5
King St. (Woodside) AB24	14	A3
King's Ct. AB24	14	B2
Auchinleck Rd.		
Kings Cres. AB24	15	E6
King's Cross AB15	23	E2
King's Cross Av. AB15	22	D3
King's Cross Rd. AB15	22	D3
King's Cross Ter. AB15	22	D3
King's Gate AB15	23	F2
Kings Rd. AB24	14	B2
Auchinleck Rd.		
Kingsford Rd. AB16	12	D6
Kingshill Av. AB15	23	E1
Kingshill Rd. AB15	23	E2
Kingshill Ter. AB15	23	E2
Kingsland Pl. AB25	4	C1
Kingswalk (Bucks.) AB21	12	C1
Kingsway (Bucks.) AB21	12	C2
Kingswells Av. (Kings.) AB15	18	D4
Kingswells Cres. (Kings.) AB15	18	D3
Kingswells Dr. (Kings.) AB15	18	C3
Kingswells Vw., Westh. AB32	16	D3
Kingswood Av. (Kings.) AB15	18	D4
Kingswood Cres. (Kings.) AB15	18	D4
Kingswood Dr. (Kings.) AB15	18	D4
Kingswood Gdns. (Kings.) AB15	18	D5
Kingswood Gro. (Kings.) AB15	18	D4
Kingswood Ms. (Kings.) AB15	18	C4
Kingswood Path (Kings.) AB15	18	D4
Kingswood Rd. (Kings.) AB15	18	D4
Kingswood Wk. (Kings.) AB15	18	D4
Kinkell Rd. AB15	22	C4
Kinmundy Av., Westh. AB32	17	E4
Kinmundy Dr., Westh. AB32	17	E4
Kinmundy Gdns., Westh. AB32	17	E4
Kinmundy Grn., Westh. AB32	17	F4
Kinnaird Pl. AB24	14	C3
Kinord Circle (Br.Don) AB22	14	D1
Kintore Gdns. AB25	24	A1
Kintore Pl.		
Kintore Pl. AB25	4	B1
Kirk Brae (Cults) AB15	28	A2
Kirk Brae Ct. (Cults) AB15	28	A2
Kirk Cres. N. (Cults) AB15	27	H2
Kirk Cres. S. (Cults) AB15	27	H2
Kirk Dr. (Cults) AB15	28	A2
Kirk Pl. (Cults) AB15	27	H2
Kirk Ter. (Cults) AB15	27	H2
Kirkbrae Av. (Cults) AB15	27	H2
Kirkbrae Dr. (Cults) AB15	27	G2
Kirkbrae Ms. (Cults) AB15	28	A2
Kirkbrae Vw. (Cults) AB15	27	H2
Kirkhill Dr. (Dyce) AB21	6	C2
Kirkhill Ind. Est. (Dyce) AB21	6	B3
Kirkhill Pl. AB11	25	E6
Kirkhill Pl. (Dyce) AB21	6	C4
Kirkhill Rd. AB11	24	D6
Kirkhill Rd. (Dyce) AB21	6	C3
Kirkside Ct., Westh. AB32	17	E4
Kirkton Av. AB21	7	E1
Kirkton Av., Westh. AB32	16	B4
Kirkton Dr. (Dyce) AB21	7	E2
Kirkton Gdns., Westh. AB32	16	B5
Kirkton Rd., Westh. AB32	16	B4
Kirkwall Av. AB16	12	B6
Kittybrewster Sq. AB25	14	B5
Kvaerner Village (Dyce) AB21	6	B2

L

Street	Page	Grid
Laburnum Wk. AB16	13	H5
Lade Cres. (Bucks.) AB21	8	C5
Ladywell Pl. AB11	25	E5
Laird Gdns. (Dane.) AB22	10	A6
Lamond Pl. AB25	14	C6
Lang Stracht AB15	22	C1
Lang Stracht AB16	22	C1
Langdykes Cres. (Co.Bay) AB12	30	D5
Langdykes Dr. (Co.Bay) AB12	30	D5
Langdykes Rd. (Co.Bay) AB12	30	D5
Langdykes Way (Co.Bay) AB12	31	E5
Langstane Pl. AB11	4	C3
Larch Rd. AB16	13	G5
Larg Dr., Westh. AB32	16	B4
Laurel Av. (Br.Don) AB22	14	A1
Laurel Dr. (Br.Don) AB22	13	H1
Laurel Gdns. (Br.Don) AB22	14	A1
Laurel Gro. (Br.Don) AB22	14	A1
Laurel La. (Br.Don) AB22	14	A1
Laurel Dr.		
Laurel Pk. (Br.Don) AB22	14	A1
Laurel Braes		
Laurel Pl. (Br.Don) AB22	13	H1
Laurel Ter. (Br.Don) AB22	13	H1
Laurel Vw. (Br.Don) AB22	14	A1
Laurel Wynd (Br.Don) AB22	13	H1
Laurelwood Av. AB25	14	B5
Laverock Way (Br.Don) AB22	10	D6
Glashieburn Way		
Laws Dr. AB12	30	A3
Laws Rd. AB12	30	A3
Lawsondale Av., Westh. AB32	17	F5
Lawsondale Dr., Westh. AB32	17	F5
Lawsondale Ter., Westh. AB32	17	F5
Lea Rig, Westh. AB32	16	B4
Leadside Rd. AB25	4	B2
Learney Pl. AB15	23	F4
Leddach Gdns., Westh. AB32	16	C4
Leddach Pl., Westh. AB32	16	C4
Leddach Rd., Westh. AB32	16	C4
Lee Cres. (Br.Don) AB22	10	A4
Lee Cres. N. (Br.Don) AB22	10	A3
Leggart Av. AB12	29	H2

Name	Page	Ref
Leggart Cres. AB12	29	H3
Leggart Pl. AB12	29	H2
Leggart Rd. AB12	29	H2
Leggart Ter. AB12	29	H2
Lemon Pl. AB24	24	D1
Park St.		
Lemon St. AB24	5	E1
Lerwick Rd. AB16	12	C6
Leslie Cres., Westh. AB32	16	C4
Leslie Rd. AB24	14	B4
Leslie Ter. AB25	14	C5
Lethen Wk. (Port.) AB12	38	C5
Lewis Ct. AB16	12	B6
Lewis Dr. AB16	12	B6
Lewis Rd. AB16	22	A1
Lewisvale, Peter. AB14	33	F3
Licklyhead Way (Dyce) AB21	7	G2
Netherview Av.		
Liddell Pl. AB21	7	F2
Lilac Pl. AB16	13	F5
Lilybank Pl. AB24	14	B4
Lime St. AB11	5	E2
Lindsay St. AB10	24	B2
Golden Sq.		
Links Pl. AB11	25	E2
Links Rd. AB11	25	E1
Links Rd. (Br.Don) AB23	15	F1
Links Rd. AB24	5	E1
Links St. AB11	25	E2
Links Vw. AB24	15	F5
Linksfield Ct. AB24	15	F4
Linksfield Gdns. AB24	15	E5
Linksfield Pl. AB24	15	E5
Linksfield Rd. AB24	15	E5
Lintmill Pl. AB16	12	D4
Lintmill Ter. AB16	12	D4
Lismore Gdns. AB16	12	B6
Taransay Rd.		
Little Belmont St. AB10	24	B2
Belmont St.		
Little Chapel St. AB10	24	A2
Chapel St.		
Littlejohn St. AB10	5	D1
Livingstone Ct. AB24	15	E3
Loanhead Pl. AB25	4	A1
Loanhead Ter. AB25	4	A1
Loanhead Wk. AB25	4	A1
Loch St. AB25	5	C1
Loch Vw., Westh. AB32	16	C3
Lochnagar Cres., Peter. AB14	33	E2
Lochnagar Rd. AB11	25	F5
Lochnagar Rd., Peter. AB14	33	E2
Lochside Av. (Br.Don) AB23	10	D4
Lochside Cres. (Br.Don) AB23	10	D4
Lochside Dr. (Br.Don) AB23	10	D4
Lochside Pl. (Br.Don) AB23	10	D4
Lochside Rd.		
Lochside Rd. (Br.Don) AB23	10	D5
Lochside Ter. (Br.Don) AB23	11	E4
Lochside Way (Br.Don) AB23	10	D4
Lochview Dr. (Br.Don) AB23	10	D4
Lochview Pl. (Br.Don) AB23	10	D4
Lochview Way (Br.Don) AB23	10	D4
Lodge Wk. AB11	24	C2
Union St.		
Logie Av. AB16	13	G2
Logie Gdns. AB16	13	G2
Logie Av.		
Logie Pl. AB16	13	F3
Logie Ter. AB16	13	F3
Loirsbank Rd. (Cults) AB15	28	A3
Loirston Av. (Co.Bay) AB12	30	D6
Loirston Cl. (Co.Bay) AB12	30	D6
Loirston Ct. (Co.Bay) AB12	30	D6
Loirston Cres. (Co.Bay) AB12	31	E6
Loirston Manor (Co.Bay) AB12	31	E6
Loirston Pl. AB11	25	E5
Loirston Pl. (Co.Bay) AB12	31	E6
Loirston Rd. AB12	31	E6
Loirston Wk. (Co.Bay) AB12	30	D5
Loirston Way (Co.Bay) AB12	30	D5
Long Wk. Pl. AB16	13	F5
Long Wk. Rd. AB16	13	F5
Long Wk. Ter. AB16	13	F5
Longcairn Gdns. (Bucks.) AB21	12	B2
Middle Brae		
Longlands Pl. AB16	13	F5
Longview Ter. AB16	12	D3
Lord Hay's Ct. AB24	15	F2
Lord Hay's Gro. (Old Aberdeen) AB24	15	E2
Lossie Pl. AB16	12	D6
Louden Pl. (Dyce) AB21	7	G2
Louisville Av. AB15	23	F4

M

Name	Page	Ref
Maberly St. AB25	4	C1
Macaulay Dr. (Craigiebuckler) AB15	22	C5
Macaulay Gdns. AB15	22	D5
Macaulay Pk. AB15	22	D5
Macaulay Pl. AB15	22	D5
Macaulay Wk. AB15	22	D5
Mackay Rd. AB12	30	A2
Mackenzie Pl. AB24	14	D4
High St.		
Mackie Pl. AB10	4	B2
Magdala Pl. AB25	24	A1
Short Loanings		
Maidencraig Pl. AB16	22	B1
Mains Circle, Westh. AB32	17	F4
Mains Ct., Westh. AB32	17	F4
Mains Dr., Westh. AB32	17	F4
Mains Gdns., Westh. AB32	17	F4
Mains Vw., Westh. AB32	17	F3
Maitlands Quay AB11	25	E4
Sinclair Rd.		
Malcolm Rd. (Bucks.) AB21	12	D1
Manor Av. AB16	13	F3
Manor Dr. AB16	13	F3
Manor Pk. Caravan Pk. AB16	13	F2
Manor Pl. (Cults) AB15	28	A3
Manor Ter. AB16	13	G3
Manor Wk. AB16	13	F3
Manse Rd. (Cults) AB15	27	G3
Mansefield Pl. AB11	24	D5
Mansefield Rd. AB11	25	E4
Maple Pl. (Co.Bay) AB12	37	F1
Marchbank Rd. (Bield.) AB15	27	F4
Marchburn Av. AB16	13	E4
Marchburn Ct. AB16	12	D3
Marchburn Ct. Rd.		
Marchburn Ct. Rd. AB16	12	D3
Marchburn Cres. AB16	13	E3
Marchburn Dr. AB16	13	E3
Marchburn Pl. AB16	13	E3
Marchburn Rd. AB16	13	E3
Marchburn Ter. AB16	13	F3
Marchburn Dr.		
Marchmont Pl. AB12	31	E5
Marchmont St. AB12	31	E5
Margaret Pl. AB10	23	H6
Margaret St. AB10	24	A2
Rose St.		
Marine Ct. AB11	24	B4
Marine Ter.		
Marine La. AB11	24	B4
Abbotsford La.		
Marine Rd. AB11	24	B4
South Crown St.		
Marine Ter. AB11	24	B4
Marine Ter. (Muchalls), Stone. AB39	40	C6
Marischal Ct. AB11	24	C2
Justice St.		
Marischal Gdns. (Bucks.) AB21	12	B2
Marischal St. AB11	5	D2
Mark Bush Ct. AB12	30	A1
Market La. AB24	14	D4
High St.		
Market St. AB11	5	D2
Market St. (Bucks.) AB21	7	F6
Marlpool Pl. (Bucks.) AB21	12	B2
Marischal Gdns.		
Marquis Rd. AB24	14	B3
Marsh Pl. (Port.) AB12	38	D4
Martins La. AB11	24	C2
Rennies Wynd		
Maryculter Br. (Maryculter) AB12	33	H4
Maryville Pk. AB15	22	D2
Anderson Dr.		
Maryville Pl. AB15	22	D2
Marywell Pk. Homes (Nigg) AB12	36	B5
Marywell St. AB11	5	C3
Mastrick Cl. AB16	13	F6
Mastrick Dr. AB16	13	E6
Mastrick Junct. AB16	13	E6
Mastrick Land AB16	13	E6
Mastrick Rd.		
Mastrick Rd. AB16	13	E6
Matthew Pk. (Bucks.) AB21	12	C1
Matthews Quay AB11	25	E3
Matthews Rd. AB12	30	A3
May Baird Av. AB25	14	B5
Ashgrove Rd.		
Mayfield Gdns. AB15	23	F4
McCombies Ct. AB10	24	A3
Union St.		
Meadow Ct. AB24	14	B2
Gordon's Mills Cres.		
Meadow La. AB24	14	C2
Meadow Pl. AB24	14	B2
Meadowlands Av., Westh. AB32	17	E2
Meadowlands Dr.		
Meadowlands Cl., Westh. AB32	17	E2
Meadowlands Cl., Westh. AB32	17	E2
Meadowlands Cres., Westh. AB32	17	E2
Meadowlands Dr., Westh. AB32	16	D2
Meadowlands Pk., Westh. AB32	16	D2
Meadowlands Pl., Westh. AB32	16	D2
Meadowlands Way, Westh. AB32	17	E2
Meadows, The, Mill. AB13	26	B4
Mealmarket St. AB24	5	D1
Mearns Quay AB11	25	E3
Mearns St. AB11	5	E2
Meikle Gdns., Westh. AB32	16	D4
Melrose Wk., Peter. AB14	32	D3
Menzies Rd. AB11	24	D4
Merkland La. AB24	15	F5
Merkland Pl. AB24	15	E5
Merkland Rd. AB24	15	E5
Merkland Rd. E. AB24	15	E5
Meston Wk. AB24	14	D4
Mid Stocket Rd. AB15	23	E1
Midchingle Rd. AB11	5	E3
Middle Brae (Bucks.) AB21	12	A2
Middle Row AB11	25	F3
Middlefield Cres. AB24	13	H3
Middlefield Pl. AB16	13	G3
Middlefield Pl. AB24	13	G3
Middlefield Ter. AB24	13	H3
Middlefield Wk. AB24	13	H4
Hilton Rd.		
Middlemuir (Bucks.) AB21	12	B3
Middlemuir Pl. (Bucks.) AB21	12	B2
Middleton Circle (Br.Don) AB22	10	A4
Middleton Cl. (Br.Don) AB22	10	A4
Middleton Cres. (Br.Don) AB22	10	A4
Middleton Dr. (Br.Don) AB22	10	A4
Middleton Gro. (Br.Don) AB22	10	A4
Middleton Path (Br.Don) AB22	10	A4
Middleton Pl. (Br.Don) AB22	10	D6
Glashieburn Way		
Middleton Rd. (Br.Don) AB22	10	A4
Middleton Ter. (Br.Don) AB22	10	A4
Middleton Way (Br.Don) AB22	10	A4
Midmar Cres. (Kings.) AB15	18	D3
Midmar Pk. (Kings.) AB15	18	D3
Midmar Vw. (Kings.) AB15	18	D4
Midmar Wk. (Kings.) AB15	18	D3
Midstocket Ms. AB15	23	E1
Mid Stocket Rd.		
Migvie Av. (Kings.) AB15	18	D3
Migvie Gdns. (Kings.) AB15	18	D3
Migvie Gro. (Kings.) AB15	18	D3
Migvie Lea (Kings.) AB15	18	D3
Mile-End Av. AB15	23	G1
Mile-End La. AB15	23	G1
Mile-End Pl. AB15	23	G1
Mill Ct. (Woodside) AB24	13	H2
Mill Lade Wynd (Br.Don) AB22	13	G1
Millarsmires End (Br.Don) AB22	10	C5
Mundurno Rd.		
Millarsmires Way AB22	10	C5
Mundurno Rd.		
Millbank La. AB25	14	C6
Millbank Pl. AB25	14	C6
Milburn St. AB11	24	B4
Milden Rd. (Cults) AB15	28	A2
Milleath Wk. (Dyce) AB21	7	G2
Balloch Way		
Miller St. AB11	5	E2
Millgrove Rd. (Bucks.) AB21	8	C5
Stoneywood Rd.		
Millhill Brae (Bucks.) AB21	8	C6

Street	Page	Grid
Millside Dr., Peter. AB14	32	D3
Millside Rd., Peter. AB14	32	C3
Millside St. AB14	32	C3
Millside Ter., Peter. AB14	32	C3
Milltimber Brae, Mill. AB13	26	A6
Milltimber Brae E., Mill. AB13	26	A6
Milton Br. (Maryculter) AB12	33	H4
Miltonfold (Bucks.) AB21	12	C1
Miltonfold Ct. (Bucks.) AB21	12	C1
Miltonfold		
Minden Cl. (Br.Don) AB23	11	F6
Minister La. AB10	24	A2
Summer St.		
Minto Av. (Altens Ind. Est.) AB12	31	F2
Minto Dr. (Altens Ind. Est.) AB12	31	F3
Minto Rd. (Altens Ind. Est.) AB12	31	F3
Moir Av. AB16	13	G4
Moir Cres. AB16	13	G4
Moir Dr. AB16	13	G5
Moir Grn. AB16	13	G4
Monach Ter. AB16	21	H1
Monduff Rd. (Muchalls), Stone. AB39	40	C6
Monearn Gdns., Mill. AB13	26	B5
Montgomery Cres. AB24	14	B2
Montgomery Rd. AB24	14	B2
Montrose Cl. (Dyce) AB21	6	C4
Montrose Dr. AB10	29	F2
Montrose Rd. (Dyce) AB21	6	C4
Montrose Way (Dyce) AB21	6	C4
Monymusk Ter. AB15	22	B4
Moor Pl. (Port.) AB12	39	E3
Moray Pl. AB15	23	E2
Morgan Rd. AB16	13	H5
Morningfield Mews AB15	23	F2
Morningfield Rd. AB15	23	E2
Morningside Av. AB10	29	F1
Morningside Cres. AB10	29	F1
Morningside Gdns. AB10	23	F6
Morningside Gro. AB10	23	F6
Morningside Rd.		
Morningside La. AB10	23	F6
Morningside Pl. AB10	23	F6
Morningside Rd. AB10	23	F6
Morningside Ter. AB10	23	F6
Morrison Dr. AB10	29	E1
Morrisons Br. (Cults) AB15	28	B3
Mortimer Dr. AB15	22	A3
Mortimer Pl. AB15	22	B3
Morven Circle, Westh. AB32	16	D4
Morven Ct. AB11	25	F5
Balnagask Circle		
Morven Cres., Westh. AB32	16	D4
Morven Dr., Westh. AB32	16	D4
Morven Gdns., Westh. AB32	16	D4
Morven Pl. AB11	24	D5
Mosman Gdns. AB24	13	H4
Mosman Pl. AB24	13	H4
Mosscroft Av., Westh. AB32	16	C6
Mosside Ct., Westh. AB32	16	D5
Brimmond Dr.		
Mosside Cres. (Port.) AB12	38	D3
Mosside Dr. (Port.) AB12	38	D3
Mosside Pl., Westh. AB32	16	D5
Brimmond Dr.		
Mosside Way (Bucks.) AB21	12	B2
Newhills Av.		
Mount Pleasant (Br.Don) AB23	15	E1
Mount St. AB25	4	B1
Mounthooly AB24	15	E6
Mounthooly Way AB24	15	E6
Mountview Gdns. AB25	24	A1
Mount St.		
Mugiemoss Ct. (Bucks.) AB21	12	D1
Mugiemoss Rd.		
Mugiemoss Rd. AB21	13	F2
Muirend Rd. (Port.) AB12	38	D3
Muirfield Pl. AB16	13	F6
Willowpark Pl.		
Muirfield Rd. AB16	13	F6
Mastrick Dr.		
Muirton Cres. (Dyce) AB21	7	G2
Mull Way AB16	22	A1
Mundurno Rd. (Br.Don) AB22	10	B6
Murcar Ind. Est. (Br.Don) AB23	11	F3
Murray Ct. AB24	13	H2
Murray Rd. (Newt.), Stone. AB39	41	E3
Murray Ter. AB11	24	B5
Myrtle Den Rd., Mill. AB13	26	D4
Myrtle Ter. (Port.) AB12	38	C4

N

Street	Page	Grid
Nellfield Pl. AB10	23	H4
Nelson Ct. AB24	15	E6
Nelson La. AB24	15	E6
Nelson St. AB24	15	E6
Ness Pl. AB16	12	D6
Netherbrae (Bucks.) AB21	12	B2
Kepplehills Rd.		
Netherby Rd. (Cults) AB15	27	H3
Netherhills Av. (Bucks.) AB21	12	B2
Netherhills Pl. (Bucks.) AB21	12	B2
Netherkirkgate AB10	24	C2
Union St.		
Nethermains Rd. (Muchalls), Stone. AB39	40	C6
Netherview Av. (Dyce) AB21	7	G3
Netherview Pl. (Dyce) AB21	7	F3
Netherview Rd. (Dyce) AB21	7	F3
Nevis Business Pk. (Br.Don) AB22	10	B6
New Pk. Pl. AB16	13	E6
New Pk. Rd. AB16	13	E6
New Pier Rd. AB11	25	F3
Newburgh Circle (Br.Don) AB22	10	B4
Newburgh Cres. (Br.Don) AB22	10	C4
Newburgh Dr. (Br.Don) AB22	10	B4
Newburgh Path (Br.Don) AB22	10	B4
Newburgh Pl. (Br.Don) AB22	10	C4
Newburgh St. (Br.Don) AB22	10	B4
Newburgh Way (Br.Don) AB22	10	B4
Newhills Av. AB21	12	B2
Newlands Av. AB10	23	G6
Newlands Cres. AB10	23	G6
Newton of Murcar Ind. Est. AB23	11	E2
Newton Pl. (Newt.), Stone. AB39	41	E3
Newton Rd.		
Newton Rd. AB16	13	G3
Newton Rd. (Dyce) AB21	6	C3
Newton Rd. (Newt.), Stone. AB39	41	E3
Newton Ter. (Bucks.) AB21	12	D1
Newtonhill Rd. (Newt.), Stone. AB39	40	D4
Nicol Pl. (Port.) AB12	39	E3
Nigg Holiday Pk. (Nigg) AB12	30	D2
Nigg Kirk Rd. AB12	30	D2
Nigg Way AB12	30	A4
Ninian Pl. (Port.) AB12	39	E2
Ninian Pl. (Dyce) AB21	6	C3
Norfolk Rd. AB10	23	G5
North Anderson Dr. AB15	13	G5
North Anderson Dr. AB16	13	G5
North Balnagask Rd. AB11	25	F4
North Deeside Rd. AB15	28	C2
North Deeside Rd., Mill. AB13	26	B6
North Deeside Rd., Peter. AB14	32	D3
North Donside Rd. (Br.Don) AB23	11	E6
North Esplanade E. AB11	5	E3
North Esplanade W. AB11	24	C4
North Grampian Circle AB11	24	D5
North St. Andrew St. AB25	24	B1
St. Andrew St.		
North Silver St. AB10	4	C2
North Sq. AB11	25	F3
North Stocket La. AB16	13	F5
Lilac Pl.		
Northburn Av. AB15	22	C3
Northburn La. AB15	22	C3
Northcote Av. AB15	22	D6
Northcote Cres. AB15	22	D6
Northcote Hill AB15	28	D1
Northcote Pk. AB15	28	D1
Northcote Rd. AB15	28	D1
Northfield Ind. Est. AB16	13	F4
Northfield Pl. AB25	4	B2
Northsea Ct. AB24	15	F3
Novar Pl. AB25	4	B1
Nursery La. AB16	13	G5
West Cairncry Rd.		

O

Street	Page	Grid
Oak Cres., Westh. AB32	16	D5
Oak Dr. (Port.) AB12	38	D5
Oakdale Ter. AB15	23	F6
St. John's Ter.		
Oakhill Cres. AB15	23	F2
Oakhill Rd. AB15	23	E2
Old Ch. Rd. AB11	24	D6
Old Coast Rd. (Port.) AB12	39	F5
Old Ferry Rd. (Bield.) AB15	27	F4
Old Ford Rd. AB11	24	C4
Old Inn Rd. (Port.) AB12	39	H2
Old Mill Rd. (Newt.), Stone. AB39	40	D4
Old Skene Rd. (Kings.) AB15	19	E6
Old Skene Rd., Westh. AB32	16	C4
Oldcroft Ct. AB16	13	G6
Castleton Dr.		
Oldcroft Pl. AB16	13	G6
Oldcroft Ter. AB16	13	G6
Oldfold Av., Mill. AB13	26	B4
Oldfold Cres., Mill. AB13	26	B4
Oldfold Dr., Mill. AB13	26	B4
Oldfold Pk., Mill. AB13	26	B4
Oldfold Wk., Mill. AB13	26	B4
Oldman Rd. AB13	33	H6
Oldmeldrum Rd. AB21	12	D1
Oldmill Rd. AB11	24	B4
Bon Accord St.		
Oldtown Pl. AB16	13	E3
Oldtown Ter. AB16	13	E3
Orchard, The AB24	14	D5
Spital Wk.		
Orchard La. AB24	15	E5
Orchard Pl.		
Orchard Pl. AB24	14	D5
Orchard Rd. AB24	15	E5
Orchard St. AB24	14	D5
Orchard Wk. AB24	14	D5
Ord St. AB15	22	D3
Oriel Ter., Peter. AB14	32	D3
Station Rd. W.		
Orkney Av. AB16	12	B6
Osborne Pl. AB25	23	G2
Oscar Pl. AB11	24	D5
Oscar Rd. AB11	24	D5
Overhill Gdns. (Br.Don) AB22	10	C6
Overhills Wk. (Br.Don) AB22	12	B2
Overton Av. (Dyce) AB21	7	G4
Overton Circle (Dyce) AB21	7	G4
Overton Cres. (Dyce) AB21	7	G4
Overton Pk. (Dyce) AB21	7	G4
Overton Wk. (Dyce) AB21	7	G4
Overton Way (Dyce) AB21	7	F4
Oyne Rd. AB15	22	C4

P

Street	Page	Grid
Paddock, The, Peter. AB14	32	D4
Palmerston Pl. AB11	24	C4
Palmerston Rd. AB11	24	C4
Park Brae (Cults) AB15	28	A3
Park La. AB24	24	D1
Princes St.		
Park Pl. AB24	24	C1
Park St.		
Park Rd. (Newt.), Stone. AB39	40	D4
Park Rd. (Cults) AB15	28	A3
Park Rd. AB24	15	F6
Park St. AB24	5	E1
Park Vw. (Br.Don) AB23	11	E6
Gordon Rd.		
Parkhead Gdns. (Bucks.) AB21	12	B2
Clashbog Pl.		
Parkhill Av. (Dyce) AB21	7	G4
Parkhill Circle (Dyce) AB21	7	F4
Parkhill Ct. (Dyce) AB21	7	G2
Balloch Way		
Parkhill Cres. (Dyce) AB21	7	G4
Parkhill Way (Dyce) AB21	7	F4
Parkside, Westh. AB32	16	D5
Parkway, The (Br.Don) AB22	9	G6
Parkway, The (Br.Don) AB23	10	B6
Parkway E. AB23	11	F5
Partan Skelly Av. (Co.Bay) AB12	30	D6
Partan Skelly Way (Co.Bay) AB12	30	D6
Patagonian Ct. AB10	24	B2
Belmont St.		
Peacocks Cl. AB24	24	C1
East N. St.		
Peat Way (Port.) AB12	38	D3
Pennan Rd. AB24	14	C2
Pentland Cres. AB11	25	F5
Pentland Pl. AB11	25	F5
Pentland Rd. AB11	25	F4
Persley Br. AB22	13	F1
Persley Cres. AB16	13	G3

Entry		
Persley Pk. Caravan Pk. (Bucks.) AB21	13	F2
Perwinnes Path (Br.Don) AB22	10	D6
Glashieburn Way		
Peterseat Dr. AB12	31	F2
Pheppie Rd. (Muchalls), Stone. AB39	40	C6
Phoenix Pl. (Bucks.) AB21	7	G6
Picardy Ct. AB10	24	A3
Rose St.		
Picktillum Av. AB25	14	B5
Picktillum Pl. AB25	14	B5
Pilot Sq. AB11	25	F3
Pinecrest Circle (Bield.) AB15	27	F2
Pinecrest Dr. (Bield.) AB15	27	E2
Pinecrest Gdns. (Bield.) AB15	27	E2
Pinecrest Wk. (Bield.) AB15	27	E3
Pinewood Av. AB15	22	B5
Pinewood Pl. (Co.Bay) AB12	31	E6
Pinewood Pl. AB15	22	B5
Pinewood Rd. AB15	22	B5
Pinewood Ter. AB15	22	C5
Piper Pl. (Port.) AB12	39	E2
Pirie's Ct. AB24	14	B4
Pirie's La. AB24	14	B4
Pitdourie Wk. (Bucks.) AB21	12	B2
Newhills Av.		
Pitfichie La. (Dyce) AB21	7	G2
Tornashean Gdns.		
Pitfichie Pl. AB21	7	G2
Pitfodels Sta. Rd. (Cults) AB15	28	D2
Pitmedden Av. (Dyce) AB21	7	F2
Pitmedden Cres. AB10	29	G2
Pitmedden Dr. (Dyce) AB21	7	F2
Pitmedden Ind. Est. (Dyce) AB21	7	E2
Pitmedden Ms. (Dyce) AB21	7	F2
Pitmedden Rd. AB10	29	G1
Pitmedden Rd. AB21	7	E1
Pitmedden Ter. AB10	29	G1
Pitmedden Way (Dyce) AB21	7	F2
Pitstruan La. AB10	23	H4
Pitstruan Ter. AB10	23	H5
Pittengullies Brae, Peter. AB14	33	F3
Pittengullies Circle, Peter. AB14	33	F3
Pittodrie La. AB24	15	E5
Pittodrie Pl. AB24	15	E5
Pittodrie St. AB24	15	E5
Plane Tree Rd. AB16	13	G5
Plover Ct. (Newt.), Stone. AB39	41	E3
Pocra Quay AB11	25	F3
Polmuir Av. AB11	24	B5
Polmuir Pl. AB11	24	B5
Polmuir Rd. AB11	24	B4
Polo Gdns. (Bucks.) AB21	7	G6
Polston Rd. AB12	33	H6
Polwarth Rd. AB11	24	C5
Poplar Rd. AB16	13	G5
Larch Rd.		
Portal Cres. AB24	14	C3
Portal Ter. AB24	14	C4
Porthill Ct. AB25	24	C1
Gallowgate		
Portland St. AB11	5	C3
Portree Av. AB16	12	C6
Poultry Mkt. La. AB10	24	C2
Queen St.		
Powis Circle AB24	14	C4
Powis Cres. AB24	14	C4
Powis La. AB25	14	C6
Powis Pl. AB25	14	C6
Powis Ter. AB25	14	C5
Poynernook Rd. AB11	5	D3
Primrosebank Av. (Cults) AB15	28	B3
Primrosebank Dr. (Cults) AB15	28	B3
Primrosehill Av. AB15	28	B3
Primrosehill Dr. AB24	14	B4
Primrosehill Gdns. AB24	14	B4
Primrosehill Pl. AB24	14	B4
Primrosehill Rd. AB15	28	B3
Prince Arthur St. AB10	4	A2
Princes St. AB24	5	D1
Princess Cres. (Dyce) AB21	7	G3
Princess Dr. (Dyce) AB21	7	G2
Princess Pl. (Dyce) AB21	7	G2
Princess Rd. (Dyce) AB21	7	G2
Princess Ter. (Dyce) AB21	7	G2
Princess Cres.		
Princess Wk. (Dyce) AB21	7	G2
Princess Rd.		

Entry		
Princess Way (Dyce) AB21	7	G2
Princess Cres.		
Printfield Ter. AB24	14	B3
Printfield Wk. AB24	14	A3
Priory Pk., Peter. AB14	33	E3
Privet Hedges AB16	13	G5
Promenade Ct. AB24	15	F4
Prospect Ct. AB11	24	C5
Prospect Ter. AB11	24	C4
Prospect Ter. (Bucks.) AB21	8	C5
Prospecthill Rd. (Bield.) AB15	27	F4
Provost Fraser Dr. AB16	13	F5
Provost Graham Av. AB15	22	B3
Provost Hogg Ct. AB11	25	F4
Provost Mitchell Circle (Br.Don) AB23	11	E2
Dubford Rd.		
Provost Rust Dr. AB16	13	F3
Provost Watt Dr. AB12	30	B1
Puffin Ct. (Newt.), Stone. AB39	41	E3

Q

Entry		
Quarry Ct. (Cults) AB15	27	G3
Quarry Pl. AB16	13	E4
Quarry Rd. (Cults) AB15	27	G3
Quarry Rd. AB16	13	E4
Queen Elizabeth II Br. AB11	24	C4
Queen St. AB10	5	D2
Queen St. (Woodside) AB24	14	A3
Queens Av. AB15	23	E4
Queens Ct. AB15	23	E4
Queen's Cross AB15	23	G3
Queens Den AB15	22	A2
Queens Gdns. AB15	23	G3
Queen's Gate AB15	23	F3
Queens La. N. AB15	23	G3
Queens La. S. AB10	23	F3
Queens La. S. AB15	23	F3
Queens Links Leisure Pk. AB24	25	E1
Queen's Rd. AB15	22	D3
Queens Ter. AB10	4	A3

R

Entry		
Raasay Gdns. AB16	22	A1
Raeburn Pl. AB25	4	B1
Raeden Av. AB15	23	E1
Raeden Ct. AB15	23	E1
Raeden Cres. AB15	23	E1
Raeden Pk. Rd. AB15	23	F1
Raeden Pl. AB15	23	E1
Raeholm Rd. (Br.Don) AB22	10	B6
Raik Rd. AB11	5	D3
Ramsay Cres. AB10	29	F1
Ramsay Gdns. AB10	29	F2
Ramsay Pl. AB10	29	F2
Rappahouse End (Br.Don) AB22	10	C6
Silverburn Rd.		
Rattray Pl. AB24	14	C2
Raxton Pl. (Dyce) AB21	7	G2
Redmoss Av. AB12	30	D3
Redmoss Pk. AB12	30	D3
Redmoss Pl. AB12	30	C3
Redmoss Rd. AB12	30	A6
Redmoss Ter. AB12	30	D3
Redmoss Wk. AB12	30	D3
Redwood Cres. (Co.Bay) AB12	37	G1
Regensburg Ct. AB16	12	D6
Regent Ct. AB24	15	F4
Regent Quay AB11	5	E2
Regent Rd. AB11	5	E3
Regent Wk. AB24	15	E4
Rennies Wynd AB11	5	D2
Richmond Ct. AB25	24	A1
Richmond Ter.		
Richmond St. AB25	4	B1
Richmond Ter. AB25	4	B1
Richmond Wk. AB25	4	B1
Richmondhill Ct. AB15	23	F2
Richmondhill Gdns. AB15	23	F1
Richmondhill Pl. AB15	23	F2
Richmondhill Rd. AB15	23	F2
Ridgeway Gro. (Dane.) AB22	10	A6
Valentine Dr.		
Ritchie Pl. AB24	14	B2
Ritchie Pl. (Muchalls), Stone. AB39	40	C6
Riverside Dr. AB10	24	A6
Riverside Dr. AB11	24	C6
Riverside Ter. AB10	23	H6

Entry		
Riverview Dr. (Dyce) AB21	7	G2
Robertson Smith Ct. AB12	30	C3
Nigg Way		
Robertson Pl., Mill. AB13	26	B5
Rockall Pl. AB11	25	E5
Rockall Rd. AB11	25	E5
Rocklands Rd. (Cults) AB15	28	B2
Rodger's Wk. AB25	4	C1
Ronaldsay Rd. AB15	22	A1
Swannay Rd.		
Ronaldsay Sq. AB15	22	A1
Swannay Rd.		
Rose Ho. (Hazlehead) AB15	22	B3
Hazlehead Rd.		
Rose Pl. AB10	24	A2
Rose St.		
Rose St. AB10	4	B2
Rosebank Gdns. AB11	24	B3
Rosebank Ter.		
Rosebank Pl. AB11	24	A4
Rosebank Ter. AB11	24	B4
Rosebery St. AB15	23	F1
Rosehill Av. AB24	13	H4
Rosehill Ct. AB16	13	G5
Rosehill Cres. AB24	14	A4
Rosehill Dr. AB24	13	H4
Rosehill Pl. AB24	14	A4
Rosehill Ter. AB24	14	A4
Rosemount Pl. AB25	4	A1
Rosemount Sq. AB25	24	A1
Richmond St.		
Rosemount Ter. AB25	4	B1
Rosemount Viaduct AB25	4	B2
Rosewell Dr. AB15	22	D2
Rosewell Gdns. AB15	22	D2
Rosewell Ho. AB15	22	D2
Rosewell Pk. AB15	22	D2
Rosewell Pl. AB15	22	D2
Rosewell Ter. AB15	22	D2
Rosewood Av. AB12	30	C3
Roslin Pl. AB24	5	E1
Roslin St. AB24	15	F6
Roslin Ter. AB24	15	E6
Ross Cres. AB16	13	F6
Rousay Dr. AB15	22	B1
Rousay Pl. AB15	22	B1
Eday Rd.		
Rousay Ter. AB15	22	B1
Rousay Dr.		
Rowan Dr., Westh. AB32	16	C5
Rowan Rd. AB16	13	H5
Rowanbank Rd. (Port.) AB12	38	D3
Royfold Cres. AB15	23	E3
Rubislaw Den Gdns. AB15	23	E3
Rubislaw Den N. AB15	23	E3
Rubislaw Den S. AB15	23	E3
Rubislaw Pk. Cres. AB15	22	D4
Rubislaw Pk. Rd. AB15	22	D4
Rubislaw Pl. AB10	4	B3
Rubislaw Ter. AB10	4	A3
Rubislaw Ter. La. AB10	4	A3
Ruby La. AB10	24	B2
North Silver St.		
Ruby Pl. AB10	24	B2
North Silver St.		
Russell Rd. AB11	24	C4
Ruthrie Ct. AB10	23	G6
Ruthrie Gdns. AB10	29	G1
Ruthrie Rd. AB10	29	G1
Ruthrie Ter. AB10	29	G1
Ruthriehill Rd. (Bucks.) AB21	8	C5
Ruthrieston Circle AB10	23	H6
Ruthrieston Cres. AB10	23	H6
Ruthrieston Gdns. AB10	29	H1
Ruthrieston Pl. AB10	23	H6
Ruthrieston Rd. AB10	23	G6
Ruthrieston Ter. AB10	29	H1

S

Entry		
St. Andrew Ct. AB25	24	B1
St. Andrew St.		
St. Andrew St. AB25	5	C1
St. Andrews Ter. (Newt.), Stone. AB39	40	D3
St. Anne's Cres. (Newt.), Stone. AB39	40	D2
St. Anne's Wynd (Newt.), Stone. AB39	40	D2
St. Catharines Wynd AB11	24	A3
Union St.		

Name	Page	Grid
St. Clair St. AB24	5	D1
St. Clement St. AB11	5	E2
St. Clements Pl. AB11	25	E2
St. Clement St.		
St. Crispin's Rd. (Newt.), Stone. AB39	40	D4
St. Devenicks Cres. (Cults) AB15	28	A3
St. Devenick's Pl. (Cults) AB15	28	A3
St. Devenick's Ter. (Cults) AB15	28	A3
St. Fitticks Rd. AB11	25	F4
St. Johns Pl. AB11	24	B3
Academy St.		
St. John's Rd. (Bucks.) AB21	12	C1
St. John's Ter. AB15	23	E6
St. John's Wk. (Newt.), Stone. AB39	40	D2
St. Machar Ct. AB24	14	B2
Montgomery Cres.		
St. Machar Dr. AB24	14	C4
St. Machar Ind. Est. AB24	14	C3
St. Machar Pl. AB24	15	E4
St. Machar Rd. AB24	14	C3
St. Margarets Pl. AB15	22	D2
St. Mary's Ct. AB24	24	B2
Union Wynd		
St. Mary's Pl. AB11	5	C3
St. Marys Pl., Peter. AB14	32	D3
North Deeside Rd.		
St. Michael's Cres. (Newt.), Stone. AB39	40	D3
St. Michael's Pl. (Newt.), Stone. AB39	40	D3
St. Michael's Rd. (Newt.), Stone. AB39	40	D3
St. Michael's Wk. (Newt.), Stone. AB39	40	D3
St. Michael's Way (Newt.), Stone. AB39	40	D3
St. Nathan's Rd. (Newt.), Stone. AB39	40	D3
St. Nicholas La. AB10	24	C2
Schoolhill		
St. Nicholas Shopping Cen. AB10	24	C2
Schoolhill		
St. Nicholas St. AB10	24	C2
Schoolhill		
St. Ninians Ct. AB24	15	E3
St. Ninians Pl. AB24	15	E2
St. Paul St. AB25	24	C1
Gallowgate		
St. Peter La. AB24	15	E6
St. Peter St. AB24	15	E6
St. Peter's Gate AB24	14	D5
St. Peter's Pl. AB24	15	E5
St. Peter's Rd. (Newt.), Stone. AB39	40	D3
St. Peters Ter., Peter. AB14	32	D3
St. Ronan's Circle, Peter. AB14	33	E2
St. Ronan's Cres., Peter. AB14	33	F2
St. Ronan's Dr., Peter. AB14	33	F3
St. Ronan's Pl., Peter. AB14	33	F3
St. Swithin Row AB10	23	G3
St. Swithin St. AB10	23	G3
St. Ternan's Rd. (Newt.), Stone. AB39	40	D4
Salisbury Ct. AB10	23	G5
Salisbury Pl. AB10	23	H5
Salisbury Ter. AB10	23	G5
Samphrey Rd. AB15	21	H2
Sanday Rd. AB15	22	C2
Sanderling Ct. (Newt.), Stone. AB39	41	E3
Sandilands Dr. AB24	14	B3
Scalpay Wk. AB16	21	H1
School Av. AB24	15	E4
School Cres., Peter. AB14	33	E3
School Dr. AB24	15	E4
School La., Peter. AB14	33	E3
School Pl. AB24	15	E4
School Dr.		
School Rd. (Cults) AB15	28	A3
School Rd. AB24	15	E4
School Rd., Peter. AB14	33	E3
School Ter. AB24	15	E4
School Wk. AB24	15	F4
Schoolhill AB10	5	C2
Schoolhill Rd. (Port.) AB12	38	D1
Sclattie Circle (Bucks.) AB21	12	B1
Sclattie Cres. (Bucks.) AB21	12	B1
Sclattie Pk. (Bucks.) AB21	12	B2
Sclattie Pl. (Bucks.) AB21	12	B2
Sclattie Wk. (Bucks.) AB21	12	B2
Scotstown Gdns. (Br.Don) AB23	15	E1
Scotstown Rd. (Br.Don) AB22	10	D6
Scotstown Rd. (Br.Don) AB23	10	D6
Scurdie Ness (Co.Bay) AB12	31	E5
Scylla Dr. (Co. Bay) AB12	37	E1
Scylla Gdns. (Co. Bay) AB12	37	E1
Scylla Gro. (Co. Bay) AB12	37	E1
Seafield Av. AB15	23	E4
Seafield Ct. AB15	23	E5
Seafield Cres. AB15	23	E5
Seafield Dr. E. AB15	23	E5
Seafield Dr. W. AB15	23	E4
Seafield Gdns. AB15	23	E5
Seafield Rd. AB15	23	E5
Seaforth Rd. AB24	15	E6
Seal Craig Gdns. AB12	30	D5
Seamount Ct. AB25	24	C1
Gallowgate		
Seamount Rd. AB25	5	D1
Seaton Av. AB24	15	E3
Seaton Cres. AB24	15	F3
Seaton Dr. AB24	15	E3
Seaton Gdns. AB24	15	E3
Seaton Ho. AB24	15	F3
Seaton Pl. AB24	15	E3
Seaton Pl. E. AB24	15	E3
Seaton Rd. AB24	15	E3
Seaton Wk. AB24	15	E3
Seaview Av. (Br.Don) AB23	11	E2
Seaview Circle (Br.Don) AB23	11	E3
Seaview Cl. (Br.Don) AB23	11	E2
Seaview Cres. (Br.Don) AB23	11	E3
Seaview Dr. (Br.Don) AB23	11	E3
Seaview Ho. AB24	15	F4
Seaview Pl. (Br.Don) AB23	11	E2
Seaview Rd. (Br.Don) AB23	15	E1
Seaview Ter. (Co.Bay) AB12	37	G1
Sedge Pl. (Port.) AB12	38	C4
Seurdie Ness AB12	31	E5
Marchmont St.		
Shapinsay Ct. AB15	22	A1
Shapinsay Rd.		
Shapinsay Rd. AB15	22	A1
Shapinsay Sq. AB15	22	A1
Shapinsay Rd.		
Shaw Circle, Westh. AB32	16	C4
Sheddocksley Dr. AB16	22	A1
Sheddocksley Rd. AB16	12	D6
Shepherd Pl. AB12	30	A2
Shetland Wk. AB16	12	C6
Shieldhill Gdns. AB12	31	E5
Shielhill Gdns. (Br.Don) AB22	10	C6
Shiprow AB11	5	D2
Shoe La. AB10	24	C1
Queen St.		
Shore Brae AB11	24	C2
Shiprow		
Shore La. AB11	24	D2
Regent Quay		
Short Loanings AB25	4	B1
Sillerton La. AB12	30	B2
Silverburn Cres. (Br.Don) AB23	11	E5
Silverburn Pl. (Br.Don) AB23	11	E5
Silverburn Rd. (Br.Don) AB22	10	C6
Simpson Rd. (Br.Don) AB23	15	E1
Sinclair Pl. AB11	25	E4
Sinclair Pl. (Co.Bay) AB12	31	E6
Sinclair Rd. AB11	24	D4
Sinclair Ter. (Co.Bay) AB12	31	E6
Skateraw Rd. (Newt.), Stone. AB39	41	E4
Skelly Rock AB12	31	E5
Skene La. AB25	4	B2
Skene Pl. AB10	24	A2
Skene St.		
Skene Pl. (Dyce) AB21	7	F3
Skene Rd. AB15	21	H2
Skene Sq. AB25	4	B1
Skene Ter. AB10	4	B2
Skye Rd. AB16	22	A1
Slains Av. (Br.Don) AB22	10	B5
Slains Circle (Br.Don) AB22	10	B5
Slains La. (Br.Don) AB22	10	C5
Slains Pl. (Br.Don) AB22	10	B6
Slains Rd. (Br.Don) AB22	10	B5
Slains St. (Br.Don) AB22	10	B5
Slains Ter. (Br.Don) AB22	10	B5
Slessor Dr. AB12	30	A4
Slessor Rd. AB12	30	A3
Sluie Dr. (Dyce) AB21	7	F2
Smithfield Ct. AB16	13	G3
Smithfield Dr. AB16	13	G3
Smithfield La. AB24	13	H3
Smithfield Rd. AB16	13	H3
Smithyhaugh Rd. AB16	12	D3
Society La. AB24	14	A3
Souter Circle, Westh. AB32	17	E4
Souter Gdns., Westh. AB32	17	E4
Souter Head Rd. AB12	30	D4
South Anderson Dr. AB10	23	G6
South Av. (Cults) AB15	28	A3
South College St. AB11	24	C3
South Constitution St. AB24	24	D1
Constitution St.		
South Crown St. AB11	24	B4
South Deeside Rd. (Maryculter) AB12	28	C4
South Esp. E. AB11	24	D4
South Esp. W. AB11	24	C4
South Grampian Circle AB11	24	D5
South Headlands Cres. (Newt.), Stone. AB39	41	E4
South Mile End AB10	24	A5
South Mt. St. AB25	4	B1
South Silver St. AB10	24	B2
Union St.		
South Sq. AB11	25	F3
South Stocket La. AB16	13	F5
Lilac Pl.		
South Wk. AB16	13	H5
Ash-hill Dr.		
Southesk Pl. (Dyce) AB21	7	F2
Spa St. AB25	4	C1
Spademill La. AB15	23	F3
Spademill Rd. AB15	23	F3
Spark Ter. (Co.Bay) AB12	37	G1
Spey Rd. AB16	13	E6
Spey Ter. AB16	13	E6
Spital AB24	14	D5
Spital Wk. AB24	14	D5
Spring Gdn. AB25	5	C1
Spring Tyne, Westh. AB32	16	B4
Springbank Pl. AB11	24	B3
Springbank St.		
Springbank St. AB11	4	C3
Springbank Ter. AB11	4	C3
Springdale Ct. (Bield.) AB15	27	F3
Springdale Cres. (Bield.) AB15	27	E3
Springdale Pk. (Bield.) AB15	27	F3
Springdale Pl. (Bield.) AB15	27	F3
Springdale Rd. (Bield.) AB15	27	E3
Springfield Av. AB15	22	D4
Springfield Gdns. AB15	22	D5
Springfield La. AB15	22	D4
Springfield Pl. AB15	22	D5
Springfield Rd. AB15	23	E5
Springhill Cres. AB16	12	D5
Springhill Rd. AB16	12	D5
Springhill Ter. (Co.Bay) AB12	37	G1
Spark Ter.		
Springhill Ter. AB16	12	D5
Square, The (Port.) AB12	39	E3
Stafford St. AB25	14	C6
Stanley Ct., Westh. AB32	16	D5
Parkside		
Stanley St. AB10	4	A3
Station Brae, Peter. AB14	33	E3
Station Ms. (Bucks.) AB21	12	D1
Oldmeldrum Rd.		
Station Rd. (Cults) AB15	28	B2
Station Rd. (Bields.) AB15	27	G4
Station Rd. (Bucks.) AB21	8	C6
Station Rd. (Dyce) AB21	7	F3
Station Rd. (Woodside) AB24	14	A2
Station Rd., Mill. AB13	26	B6
Station Rd. E., Mill. AB13	26	B6
Station Rd. E., Peter. AB14	33	E4
Station Rd. S., Peter. AB14	32	D4
Station Rd. W., Peter. AB14	32	D3
Stell Rd. AB11	5	D3
Stevenson Ct. AB25	24	A2
Upper Denburn		
Stevenson St. AB25	4	B2
Stewart Cres. AB16	13	E4
Stewart Pk. Ct. AB24	13	H4
Stewart Pk. Pl. AB24	13	H4
Stewart Ter. AB16	13	E4

Name	Page	Grid
Stirling St. AB11	24	C2
Guild St.		
Stocket Gra. AB16	13	G6
Stocket Par. AB16	13	F5
Stockethill Av. AB16	13	G6
Stockethill Cres.		
Stockethill Ct. AB16	13	G5
Stockethill Cres. AB16	13	G6
Stockethill La. AB16	13	G5
Oldcroft Ter.		
Stockethill Pl. AB16	13	G6
Castleton Dr.		
Stockethill Sq. AB16	13	G6
Stockethill Cres.		
Stockethill Way AB16	13	G5
Oldcroft Ter.		
Stonehaven Rd. AB12	38	B5
Stoneyhill Ter. AB12	37	G1
Stoneyton Ter. (Bucks.) AB21	8	B6
Stoneywood Pk. (Dyce) AB21	7	G6
Stoneywood Pk. N. (Dyce) AB21	7	G5
Stoneywood Rd. (Dyce) AB21	8	C5
Stoneywood Ter. (Bucks.) AB21	7	G6
Stornoway Cres. AB16	12	B6
Strachan Pl. AB16	13	F3
Fowler Av.		
Straik Pl., Westh. AB32	16	C5
Straik Rd., Westh. AB32	16	D5
Stranathro Ter. (Muchalls), Stone. AB39	40	C6
Strathbeg Pl. (Br.Don) AB22	14	D1
Davan Pk.		
Strathburn St. AB12	30	D5
Strathmore Dr. AB16	13	E5
Strawberry Bk. Par. AB11	4	B3
Stroma Ter. AB16	22	A1
Stronsay Av. AB15	22	C2
Stronsay Cres. AB15	22	C1
Stronsay Dr. AB15	22	C2
Stronsay Pl. AB15	22	C2
Sugarhouse La. AB11	24	D2
Mearns St.		
Sumburgh Cres. AB16	12	B6
Summer Pl. (Dyce) AB21	7	F3
Summer St. AB10	4	B2
Summer St. (Woodside) AB24	14	A3
Summerfield Pl. AB24	24	C1
Summerfield Ter.		
Summerfield Ter. AB24	5	D1
Summerhill Ct. AB15	22	D1
Summerhill Rd.		
Summerhill Cres. AB15	22	C1
Summerhill Dr. AB15	22	C1
Summerhill Rd. AB15	22	D1
Summerhill Ter. AB15	22	C2
Sunert Rd., Mill. AB13	26	D5
Sunnybank Pl. AB24	14	D5
Sunnybank Rd. AB24	14	D5
Sunnybrae (Bucks.) AB21	12	B2
Sunnyside Av. AB24	14	C5
Sunnyside Gdns. AB24	14	D5
Sunnyside Rd. AB24	14	C5
Sunnyside Ter. AB24	14	D5
Sunnyside Wk. AB24	14	D5
Sunnybank Pl.		
Swannay Rd. AB15	22	A1
Swannay Sq. AB15	22	A1
Shapinsay Rd.		
Sycamore Pl. AB11	24	B5

T

Name	Page	Grid
Talisman Dr. AB10	29	E2
Talisman Rd. AB10	29	E2
Talisman Wk. AB10	29	E1
Tanfield Av. AB24	14	B3
Tanfield Ct. AB24	14	B3
Tanfield Wk.		
Tanfield Wk. AB24	14	B3
Taransay Ct. AB16	12	C6
Taransay Cres. AB16	12	C6
Taransay Rd. AB16	21	H1
Tarbothill Rd. AB22	14	C1
Tay Rd. AB16	13	E5
Tedder Rd. AB24	14	C3
Tedder St. AB24	14	C3
Tern Ct. (Newt.), Stone. AB39	41	E3
Tern Pl. AB23	11	E3
Tern Rd. (Co. Bay) AB12	30	D6

Name	Page	Grid
Teviot Rd. AB16	12	D6
Theatre La. AB11	24	D2
Regent Quay		
Thistle Ct. AB10	4	B2
Thistle Dr. (Port.) AB12	39	E2
Thistle La. AB10	4	B2
Thistle Pl. AB10	4	B3
Thistle Rd. (Dyce) AB21	6	C4
Thistle St. AB10	4	B3
Thomas Glover Pl. (Br.Don) AB22	14	D1
Thoms Ct. AB24	14	D4
High St.		
Thoms Pl. AB24	14	D4
High St.		
Thomson St. AB25	4	A1
Thomson St. La. AB25	23	H1
Loanhead Pl.		
Thorngrove Av. AB15	23	F5
Thorngrove Cres. AB15	23	F5
Thorngrove Pl. AB15	23	F5
Tillydrone Av. AB24	14	D3
Tillydrone Ct. AB24	14	C2
Tillydrone Rd. AB24	14	C3
Tillydrone Ter. AB24	14	C3
Tiree Cres. AB16	22	A1
Todhead Gdns. AB12	31	E5
Todlaw Wk. (Dyce) AB21	7	G2
Tollohill Cres. AB12	30	C2
Tollohill Dr. AB12	30	C2
Tollohill Gdns. AB12	30	C2
Tollohill La. AB12	30	B2
Tollohill Pl. AB12	30	C2
Tollohill Sq. AB12	30	B2
Tornashean Gdns. (Dyce) AB21	7	G2
Towerview La., Peter. AB14	32	D2
Towerview Pk., Peter. AB14	32	D2
Towerview Rd., Peter. AB14	32	D2
Towerview Wk., Peter. AB14	32	D2
Towerview Way, Peter. AB14	32	D2
Towerview Wynd, Peter. AB14	32	D2
Towerview Rd.		
Trinity Ct., Westh. AB32	17	E4
Trinity La. AB11	24	C2
Exchange St.		
Trinity Quay AB11	5	D2
Trinity St. AB11	24	C2
Rennies Wynd		
Tulloch Pk. (Bucks.) AB21	12	B2
Newhills Av.		
Tullos Circle AB11	24	D5
Tullos Cres. AB11	25	E5
Tullos Pl. AB11	25	E5
Turnberry Ct. (Br.Don) AB22	10	C5
Turnberry Cres. (Br.Don) AB22	10	D5
Turnberry Gdns. (Br.Don) AB22	10	D5
Turnstone Ct. (Newt.), Stone. AB39	41	E3
Two Mile Cross AB10	29	G2

U

Name	Page	Grid
Ugie Pl. AB16	13	E5
Uist Rd. AB16	21	H1
Union Br. AB11	24	B2
Union St.		
Union Glen AB11	4	B3
Union Glen Ct. AB11	24	A3
Union Glen		
Union Gro. AB10	4	A3
Union Gro. Ct. AB10	23	G4
Union Gro.		
Union Gro. La. AB10	23	H4
Union Row AB11	4	B3
Union Row (Dyce) AB21	7	F3
Union St. AB11	4	B3
Union St. AB11	4	B3
Union Ter. AB10	4	C2
Union Wynd AB10	4	B2
University Ct. (Bucks.) AB21	12	B2
University Rd. AB24	14	D4
Upper Denburn AB25	4	B2
Upper Fairburn Rd. AB21	7	E5
Upper Mastrick Way AB16	13	E5
Upperkirkgate AB10	5	D2
Urquhart La. AB24	15	E6
Urquhart Pl. AB24	15	F6
Urquhart Rd. AB24	15	E6
Urquhart St. AB24	15	F6
Urquhart Ter. AB24	15	F6

Name	Page	Grid
Usan Ness AB12	31	E5

V

Name	Page	Grid
Valentine Cres. (Dane.) AB22	10	B6
Valentine Dr. (Dane.) AB22	10	A6
Valentine Rd. (Br.Don) AB22	10	A5
Valley Cres. AB12	30	C2
Valley Gdns. AB12	30	B2
Victoria Br. AB11	5	E3
Victoria Rd. AB11	24	D4
Victoria St. AB10	4	B2
Victoria St. (Dyce) AB21	7	F3
View Ter. AB25	4	A1
Viewfield Av. AB15	23	E5
Viewfield Cres. AB15	23	E5
Viewfield Gdns. AB15	22	D5
Viewfield Rd. AB15	22	D5
Viking Pl. (Port.) AB12	39	E2
Villagelands Rd. (Newt.), Stone. AB39	41	E4
Virginia St. AB11	24	C2
Justice St.		
Virginia St. AB11	5	D2

W

Name	Page	Grid
Wagley Ct. (Bucks.) AB21	12	B2
Newhills Av.		
Wagley Par. (Bucks.) AB21	12	B2
Wagley Pl. (Bucks.) AB21	12	B2
Wagrills La. AB24	14	D4
High St.		
Wales La. AB11	24	D2
Mearns St.		
Wales St. AB11	5	E1
Walker La. AB11	24	D4
Walker Pl. AB11	24	C4
Walker Rd. AB11	24	C5
Wallace Ho. AB15	22	B3
Hazlehead Rd.		
Wallacebrae Av. (Dane.) AB22	9	G6
Wallacebrae Cres. (Dane.) AB22	9	H6
Wallacebrae Dr. (Dane.) AB22	9	H6
Wallacebrae Gdns. (Br.Don) AB22	9	H6
Wallacebrae Path (Dane.) AB22	9	G6
Wallacebrae Ter.		
Wallacebrae Pl. (Dane.) AB22	9	H6
Wallacebrae Rd. (Dane.) AB22	9	H6
Wallacebrae Ter. (Dane.) AB22	9	G6
Wallacebrae Wk. (Dane.) AB22	9	G6
Wallacebrae Wynd (Dane.) AB22	9	H6
Wallfield Cres. AB25	4	A2
Wallfield Pl. AB25	4	A2
Walton Rd. (Bucks.) AB21	6	C3
Walton Rd. (Dyce) AB21	6	C6
Wapping St. AB11	5	C2
Wardhead Pl. AB16	12	C6
Watchman Brae (Bucks.) AB21	12	B3
Water La. AB11	24	D2
Mearns St.		
Waterloo Quay AB11	5	E2
Waterton Rd. (Bucks.) AB21	8	C5
Watson La. AB25	4	A1
Watson St. AB25	4	A1
Waulkmill Cres. AB16	13	E4
Waulkmill Rd. AB16	12	D4
Wavell Cres. AB24	14	B2
Waverley La. AB10	4	B2
Waverley Pl. AB10	4	B3
Weavers Row AB16	13	E4
Byron Cres.		
Webster Rd. AB12	30	A2
Weighhouse Sq. AB11	24	D2
Virginia St.		
Wellbrae Ter. AB15	23	E5
Wellgrove Cres., Westh. AB32	16	C5
Wellgrove Dr., Westh. AB32	16	C5
Wellgrove Rd.		
Wellgrove Rd., Westh. AB32	16	C5
Wellheads Cres. (Dyce) AB21	7	F5
Wellheads Dr. (Dyce) AB21	7	F5
Wellheads Ind. Est. (Dyce) AB21	7	F4
Wellheads Pl. (Dyce) AB21	7	F5
Wellheads Rd. (Dyce) AB21	7	G5
Wellheads Ter. (Dyce) AB21	7	F6
Wellheads Way (Dyce) AB21	7	F5
Wellington Brae AB24	24	C4
Wellington Br. AB11	24	C5
Wellington Circle (Altens) AB12	30	C4
Wellington Pl. AB11	5	C3

Wellington Rd. AB11	24	C5	Westhill Gra., Westh. AB32	16	C4	Willowpark Cres. AB16	22	D1
Wellington Rd. AB12	30	B6	Westhill Hts., Westh. AB32	16	C3	Willowpark Pl. AB16	13	F6
Wellington St. AB11	25	E2	Westhill Rd., Westh. AB32	17	F4	Willowpark Rd. AB16	13	F6
Wellside Av. (Kings.) AB15	18	D3	Westholme Av. AB15	22	D3	Windford Rd. AB16	22	A1
Wellside Circle (Kings.) AB15	19	E3	Westholme Cres. N. AB15	22	C3	Windford Sq. AB16	22	B1
Wellside Cl. (Kings.) AB15	19	E3	Westholme Cres. S. AB15	22	C3	Windmill Brae AB11	5	C2
Wellside End (Kings.) AB15	19	E3	Westholme Ter. AB15	22	C3	Windmill La. AB11	24	B2
Wellside Gdns. (Kings.) AB15	18	D3	Westray Cres. AB15	22	C1	*Windmill Brae*		
Wellside Pk. (Kings.) AB15	19	E3	Westray Rd. AB15	22	C1	Windsor Pl. AB10	24	A2
Wellside Pl. (Kings.) AB15	19	E3	Westwood Cres., Westh. AB32	16	D4	*Victoria St.*		
Wellside Rd. (Kings.) AB15	19	E3	Westwood Dr., Westh. AB32	16	D4	Windyedge Ct. (Newt.), Stone. AB39	40	D4
Wellside Wk. (Kings.) AB15	19	E3	Westwood Gro., Westh. AB32	16	D4	Wingate Pl. AB24	14	C3
Wellside Wynd (Kings.) AB15	19	E3	Westwood Pl., Westh. AB32	16	D4	Wingate Rd. AB24	14	C3
Wellwood Ter. (Cults) AB15	28	B2	Westwood Wk., Westh. AB32	16	D4	Wood St. AB11	25	F4
West Cairncry Rd. AB16	13	F5	Westwood Way, Westh. AB32	16	D4	Wood St. La. AB11	25	F4
West Craibstone St. AB11	24	B3	Whin Pk. Pl. AB16	13	E5	Woodburn Av. AB15	22	C4
Bon Accord Ter.			Whin Pk. Rd. AB16	13	E5	Woodburn Cres. AB15	22	B4
West Cults Rd. (Cults) AB15	27	H4	Whinhill Gdns. AB11	24	B5	Woodburn Gdns. AB15	22	C4
West Mt. St. AB25	4	B1	Whinhill Gate AB11	24	B4	Woodburn Pl. AB15	22	C4
West N. St. AB24	5	D1	Whinhill Rd. AB11	24	A5	Woodcroft Av. (Br.Don) AB22	10	A2
West Tullos Ind. Est. AB12	30	C1	Whinpark Circle (Port.) AB12	38	D4	Woodcroft Gdns. (Br.Don) AB22	10	A2
West Tullos Rd. AB12	30	C1	Whitehall Ms. AB25	23	H2	Woodcroft Gro. (Br.Don) AB22	10	A2
Westburn Ct. AB25	24	A1	*Whitehall Pl.*			Woodcroft Rd. (Br.Don) AB22	10	A2
Westburn Rd.			Whitehall Pl. AB25	4	A2	Woodcroft Wk. (Br.Don) AB22	10	A2
Westburn Cres. AB25	14	A6	Whitehall Rd. AB25	23	G2	*Woodcroft Av.*		
Westburn Dr. AB25	14	A5	Whitehall Ter. AB25	4	A2	Woodend Av. AB15	22	B2
Westburn Pk. AB25	14	B6	Whitehills Cres. (Co.Bay) AB12	30	D6	Woodend Cres. AB15	22	B2
Westburn Rd. AB16	23	E1	Whitehills Ri. (Co.Bay) AB12	30	D6	Woodend Dr. AB15	22	B2
Westburn Rd. AB25	4	A1	Whitehills Way (Co.Bay) AB12	30	D6	Woodend Pl. AB15	22	B3
Westdyke Av., Westh. AB32	16	C5	Whitehouse St. AB10	4	B2	Woodend Rd. AB15	22	B2
Westdyke Cl., Westh. AB32	16	C4	Whiteland Rd. (Newt.), Stone. AB39	41	E4	Woodend Ter. AB15	22	C2
Westdyke Ct., Westh. AB32	16	B5	*Murray Rd.*			Woodhill Ct. AB16	13	G6
Westdyke Dr., Westh. AB32	16	B5	Whitemyres Av. AB16	22	C1	*Castleton Dr.*		
Westdyke Gdns., Westh. AB32	16	B5	Whitemyres Pl. AB16	22	C1	Woodhill Pl. AB15	23	E2
Westdyke Pl., Westh. AB32	16	C5	Whiteashes (Kings.) AB15	18	D6	Woodhill Rd. AB15	23	E2
Westdyke Ter., Westh. AB32	16	B5	*Fairley Rd.*			Woodhill Ter. AB15	23	E1
Westdyke Wk., Westh. AB32	16	C5	Whitestripes Av. (Br.Don) AB22	10	A4	Woodlands Dr. AB21	6	C3
Westdyke Way, Westh. AB32	16	B5	Whitestripes Cl. (Br.Don) AB22	10	B5	Woodlands Rd. AB21	6	C3
Western Rd. AB24	14	B3	Whitestripes Cres. (Br.Don) AB22	10	B5	Woodside Rd. AB23	11	E4
Westerton Cres. AB16	12	D3	Whitestripes Dr. (Br.Don) AB22	10	A4	Woodstock Rd. AB15	23	E2
Westerton Pl. (Cults) AB15	28	B3	Whitestripes Path (Br.Don) AB22	10	B5	Woolmanhill AB25	4	C2
Westerton Pl. AB16	13	F3	Whitestripes Pl. (Br.Don) AB22	10	B5	Wright's & Cooper's Pl. AB24	14	D4
Marchburn Dr.			Whitestripes Rd. (Br.Don) AB22	9	H4	*High St.*		
Westerton Rd. (Cults) AB15	28	B2	Whitestripes St. (Br.Don) AB22	10	B5	Wrights Wk., Westh. AB32	17	E4
Westfield Gdns., Westh. AB32	16	D4	Whitestripes Way (Br.Don) AB22	10	B5	Wynford La., Westh. AB32	17	F4
Westfield Rd. AB25	4	A2	Wilkie Av. AB16	13	G3			
Westfield Ter. AB25	4	A2	Willow Wynd (Port.) AB12	38	C4	**Y**		
Westgate (Bucks.) AB21	12	B2	Willowbank Rd. AB11	24	A4	York Pl. AB11	25	E2
Westhill Business Pk., Westh. AB32	16	D5	Willowdale Pl. AB24	5	D1	York St. AB11	25	E2
Westhill Cres., Westh. AB32	16	D4	Willowgate Cl. AB11	24	A3	Ythan Rd. AB16	12	D6
Westhill Dr., Westh. AB32	17	E4	*Hardgate*					

Name	Page	Grid
Aberchirder	50	B2
Aberdeen	53	G3
Aberdeen Airport	53	F2
Aberlemno	54	D4
Aboyne	52	C4
Achath	53	E2
Affleck	53	F1
Aldie	51	F4
Aldivalloch	52	A1
Aldunie	52	A1
Alford	52	C2
Allancreich	52	C4
Allardice	55	G2
Altens	53	G3
Alyth	54	A5
Arbirlot	55	D5
Arbroath	55	E5
Arbuthnott	55	G2
Ardallie	51	F4
Ardgowse	52	D2
Ardiecow	50	A1
Ardlair	52	C1
Ardler	54	A5
Ardo	51	D4
Ardoyne	53	D1
Arnhall	55	E3
Arrat	55	E4
Arthrath	51	E4
Arthurstone	54	A5
Artrochie	51	F4
Ascreavie	54	B4
Asloun	52	C2
Aucharnie	50	B3
Auchattie	53	D4
Auchenblae	55	F2
Auchinhira	50	B3
Auchintoul	52	C2
Aberdeenshire		
Auchintoul	50	B2
Aberdeenshire		
Auchiries	51	F4
Auchleven	52	D1
Auchlunies	53	F4
Auchmacoy	51	E4
Auchmair	52	A1
Auchmithie	55	E5
Auchmull	55	D2
Auchnacree	54	C3
Auchnagatt	51	E3
Aucholzie	52	A4
Auchorrie	53	D3
Auchronie	52	B5
Auchtertyre	54	A5
Auds	50	B1
Aulton	52	D1
Auquhorthies	53	F1
B		
Backburn	50	A4
Backfolds	51	F2
Backhill	50	C4
Backhill of Clackriach	51	E3
Backhill of Trustach	52	D4
Badenscoth	50	B4
Badenyon	52	A2
Bainshole	50	B4
Balbithan	53	E2
Balchers	50	C2
Baldovie	54	B4
Balendoch	54	A5
Balfield	54	D3
Balfour	52	C4
Balgove	50	D4
Balgreen	50	C2
Balhalgardy	53	E1
Balhary	54	A5
Balkeerie	54	B5
Ballater	52	A4
Ballaterach	52	B4
Balloch	54	B4
Ballochan	52	C4
Ballogie	52	C4
Balmadies	54	D5
Balmedie	53	G2
Balnaboth	54	B3
Balnamoon	54	D3
Balthangie	50	D2
Bamff	54	A4
Banchory	53	E4
Banchory-Devenick	53	G3
Banff	50	B1
Bankhead	52	D2
Aberdeenshire		
Bankhead	53	D3
Aberdeenshire		
Bankhead *Aberdeen*	53	F3
Barnhead	55	E4
Barthol Chapel	50	D4
Baulds	52	D4
Bearnie	51	E4
Beggshill	50	A4
Belhelvie	53	G2
Belhinnie	52	B1
Bellabeg	52	A2
Bellaty	54	A4
Belliehill	55	D3
Benholm	55	G3
Benthoul	53	F3
Berryhillock	50	A1
Bieldside	53	F3
Birkenhills	50	C3
Birkhall	52	A4
Birse	52	C4
Birsemore	52	C4
Blackbraes	53	F2
Blackburn	53	F2
Blackchambers	53	E2
Blackdog	53	G2
Blackford	50	B4
Blackhill *Aberdeenshire*	51	F2
Blackhill *Aberdeenshire*	51	F3
Blackness	53	D4
Blacktop	53	F3
Blairshinnoch	50	B1
Blairydryne	53	E4
Blairython Cottage	53	G1
Blindburn	51	E4
Boddam	51	G3
Bogbrae	51	F4
Bogfern	52	C3
Bogfields	52	C3
Bogfold	50	D2
Boghead	50	B2
Bogniebrae	50	A3
Bograxie	53	E2
Bogston	52	A3
Bogton	50	B2
Bolshan	55	E4
Bonnykelly	51	D2
Bonnyton	50	B4
Aberdeenshire		
Bonnyton *Angus*	55	E4
Borrowfield	53	F4
Boultenstone Hotel	52	B2
Boyndie	50	B1
Boysack	55	E5
Brackens	50	C2
Bracklach	52	A1
Bracklamore	50	D2
Bracobrae	50	A2
Braedownie	54	A2
Braefoot	50	C3
Braehead of Lunan	55	E4
Brathens	53	D4
Brechin	55	E3
Brideswell	50	A4
Bridge o' Ess	52	C4
Bridge of Alford	52	C2
Bridge of Bogendreip	53	D4
Bridge of Canny	53	D4
Bridge of Craigisla	54	A4
Bridge of Dee	53	D4
Bridge of Don	53	G3
Bridge of Dun	55	E4
Bridge of Dye	53	D5
Bridge of Feugh	53	D4
Bridge of Gairn	52	A4
Bridge of Muchalls	53	F4
Bridge of Muick	52	A4
Bridgend	50	A4
Aberdeenshire		
Bridgend *Angus*	54	D3
Bridgend of Lintrathen	54	A4
Bridgeton	52	C2
Broadsea	51	E1
Broomfield	51	E4
Broomhead	51	E1
Brownhill	51	D3
Bruntland	52	B1
Buchanhaven	51	G3
Bucksburn	53	F3
Bulwark	51	E3
Burn Farm	55	E2
Burnend	50	D3
Burnhaven	51	G3
Burnhervie	53	E2
Burnside *Aberdeenshire*	53	E2
Burnside *Angus*	54	D4
C		
Cabrach	52	A1
Cairnbeathie	52	C3
Cairnbrogie	53	F1
Cairnbulg	51	F1
Cairness	51	F1
Cairnhill *Aberdeenshire*	53	G1
Cairnhill *Aberdeenshire*	50	B4
Cairnie	53	F3
Cairnorrie	51	D3
Caldhame	54	C5
Cambus o'May	52	B4
Cammachmore	53	G4
Candacraig	52	A4
Canterbury	50	A2
Carcary	55	E4
Cardno	51	E1
Careston	54	D3
Carmont	53	F5
Carmyllie	54	D5
Carnichal	51	E2
Carnousie	50	B2
Carrot	54	C5
Castleton	50	C2
Aberdeenshire		
Castleton *Angus*	54	B5
Catterline	55	G2
Cauldcots	55	E5
Causeyend	53	G2
Chapel Hill	51	F4
Chapel of Garioch	53	E1
Chapelton	53	F5
Aberdeenshire		
Chapelton *Angus*	55	E5
Charleston	54	B5
Charlestown	51	F1
Aberdeenshire		
Charlestown *Aberdeen*	53	G3
Clachnabrain	54	B3
Clatt	52	C1
Clatterin Brig	55	E2
Clinterty	53	F2
Clochtow	51	F4
Clockhill	51	D3
Clola	51	F3
Clova *Aberdeenshire*	52	B1
Clova *Angus*	54	B2
Clovenstone	53	E2
Cloverhill	53	G2
Clune *Moray*	50	A1
Clunie	50	B2
Cobairdy	50	A3
Coburty	51	E1
Coldwells	51	G3
Collieston	51	F5
Colliston	55	E5
Collmuir	52	C3
Collynie	50	D4
Colpy	50	B4
Comers	53	D3
Conland	50	B3
Cononsyth	55	D5
Contlaw	53	F3
Cookney	53	F4
Cookston	51	E4
Coralhill	51	F1
Cordach	52	D4
Cornhill	50	A2
Corrachree	52	B3
Corse	50	B3
Corse of Kinnoir	50	A3
Corsindae	53	D3
Cortachy	54	B4
Cothall	53	F2
Cottown *Aberdeenshire*	52	C1
Cottown *Aberdeenshire*	50	D3
Cottown *Aberdeenshire*	53	E2
Coull	52	C3
Coupar Angus	54	A5
Cove Bay	53	G3
Cowie	53	F5
Coynach	52	B3
Craibstone	53	F2
Craichie	54	C5
Craigculter	51	E2
Craigdam	50	D4
Craigearn	53	E2
Craigellie	51	F1
Craigie	53	G2
Craigie Brae	51	D4
Craiglug	53	F4
Craigmaud	51	D2
Craigmyle House	52	D3
Craigo	55	E3
Craigton *Aberdeen*	53	F3
Craigton *Angus*	54	B4
Craik	52	B1
Cranna	50	B2
Craskins	52	C3
Crathes	53	E4
Crawton	55	G2
Crichie	51	E3
Crimond	51	F2
Crimonmogate	51	F2
Crofts of Haddo	50	D4
Crombie Mill	54	D5
Cromblet	50	C4
Cross of Jackson	50	C4
Crossroads	53	E4
Crovie	50	D1
Cruchie	50	A3
Cruden Bay	51	F4
Culdrain	50	A4
Cullen	50	A1
Culsh	52	A4
Cultercullen	53	G1
Cults *Aberdeenshire*	50	A4
Cults *Aberdeen*	53	F3
Culvie	50	A2
Cuminestown	50	D2
Cushnie	50	C1
Cuttyhill	51	F2
D		
Dalbog	55	D2
Dalfad	52	A3
Dalmadilly	53	E2
Danestone	53	G2
Darnabo	50	C3
Darnford	53	E4
Darra	50	C3
Dartfield	51	F2
Davan	52	B3
Daviot	53	E1
Deecastle	52	B4
Delfrigs	53	G1
Delphorrie	52	B2
Denend	50	A4
Denhead *Aberdeenshire*	53	E2
Denhead *Aberdeenshire*	51	E1
Denhead of Arbirlot	55	D5
Denmill	53	F2
Denmoss	50	B3
Denside	53	F4
Dinnet	52	B4
Dorsell	52	C2
Douglastown	54	C5
Dounepark	50	C1
Douneside	52	B3
Downies	53	G4
Drumblade	50	A3
Drumblair	50	B3
Drumgley	54	C5
Drumhead	52	D4
Drumlasie	52	D3
Drumlithie	53	E5
Drumnagorrach	50	A2
Drumoak	53	E4
Drums	53	G1
Drumwhindle	51	E4
Drunkendub	55	E5
Drymuir	51	E3
Dubford	50	C1
Dubton	55	D4
Dulax	52	A2
Dun	55	E4
Duncanston	52	C1
Dunecht	53	E3
Dunlappie	55	D3
Dunnichen	54	D5
Durno	53	E1
Dyce	53	F2
Dykehead	52	B3
Dykelands	55	F3
Dykends	54	A4
Dykeside	50	C3
E		
Earlsford	50	D4
Eassie and Nevay	54	B5
East Auchronie	53	F3
East Cairnbeg	55	F2
East Davoch	52	B3

East Learney	52	D3
East Mains	53	D4
Easter Knox	55	D5
Easter Lednathie	54	B3
Easter Ord	53	F3
Easter Tulloch	55	F2
Easter Whyntie	50	B1
Ecclesgreig	55	F3
Echt	53	E3
Edinbanchory	52	B2
Edzell	55	D3
Ellon	51	E4
Elrick *Aberdeenshire*	53	F3
Elrick *Moray*	52	B1
Errollston	51	F4
Esslemont	53	G1
Ethie Mains	55	E5

F

Fairley	53	F3
Farmtown	50	A2
Farnell	55	E4
Fattahead	50	B2
Fawsyde	55	G2
Feith-hill	50	B3
Fern	54	C3
Fernybank	54	D2
Ferryden	55	F4
Fetterangus	51	E2
Fettercairn	55	E2
Fetternear House	53	E2
Feus of Caldhame	55	E3
Fichlie	52	B2
Finavon	54	C4
Findon	53	G4
Fingask	53	E1
Finnygaud	50	B2
Fintry	50	C2
Finzean	52	C4
Fisherford	50	B4
Fishtown of Usan	55	F4
Fleuchats	52	A3
Flushing	51	F3
Folla Rule	50	C4
Forbestown	52	A2
Fordoun	55	F2
Fordyce	50	A1
Forfar	54	C4
Fortrie	50	B3
Foulzie	50	C1
Foveran House	53	G1
Fraserburgh	51	E1
Frendraught	50	B3
Friockheim	55	D5
Fyvie	50	C4

G

Gallery	55	E3
Gallowfauld	54	C5
Gamrie	50	C1
Gannochy	55	E2
Gardenstown	50	C1
Garlogie	53	E3
Garmond	50	D2
Gartly	50	A4
Garvock	55	F2
Gask *Aberdeenshire*	51	F3
Gask *Aberdeenshire*	50	C3
Gateside *Aberdeenshire*	52	D2
Gateside *Angus*	54	C5
Glamis	54	B5
Glanderston	52	C1
Glascorrie	52	A4
Glashmore	53	E3
Glassel	53	D4
Glasterlaw	55	D4
Glenarm	54	B3
Glenbervie	53	E5
Glencat	52	C4
Glencuie	52	B2
Glendoll Lodge	54	A2
Glendye Lodge	52	D5
Glenhead Farm	54	A3
Glenkindie	52	B2
Glenlee	52	B5
Glenmoy	54	C3
Glenogil	54	C3
Glenprosen Village	54	B3
Glenquiech	54	C3
Glensaugh	55	E2
Glenshalg	52	C3
Glenton	52	D1

Gordonstown *Aberdeenshire*	50	A2
Gordonstown *Aberdeenshire*	50	C4
Gorrachie	50	C2
Gourdas	50	C3
Gourdon	55	G2
Gowanhill	51	F1
Grainhow	51	D3
Grantlodge	53	E2
Greendams	52	D4
Greenhall	52	D1
Greenheads	51	F4
Greenlaw	50	B2
Greenmyre	50	D4
Greystone	54	D5
Guthrie	55	D4
Guynd	55	D5

H

Hardgate	53	E3
Hatton	51	F4
Hatton Castle	50	C3
Hatton of Fintray	53	F2
Hattoncrook	53	F1
Haughs	50	A3
Hayhillock	54	D5
Hazelhead	53	F3
Heathcot	53	F3
Heugh-head *Aberdeenshire*	52	A2
Heugh-head *Aberdeenshire*	52	C4
Hillbrae *Aberdeenshire*	50	B3
Hillbrae *Aberdeenshire*	53	E1
Hillbrae *Aberdeenshire*	50	D4
Hillhead of Auchentumb	51	E2
Hillhead of Cocklaw	51	F3
Hillockhead *Aberdeenshire*	52	A3
Hillockhead *Aberdeenshire*	52	B2
Hillside *Aberdeenshire*	53	G4
Hillside *Angus*	55	F3
Hilton Croft	51	E4
Hirn	53	E3
Hoggie	50	A1
Horniehaugh	54	C3
Howe of Teuchar	50	C3
Huntly	50	A3
Hythie	51	F2

I

Idvies	54	D5
Inch of Arnhall	55	E2
Inchbare	55	E3
Inchbraoch	55	F4
Inchgrundle	54	C2
Inchmarlo	53	D4
Inchnabobart	52	A5
Inchock	55	E5
Inkhorn	51	E4
Insch	52	D1
Inverallochy	51	F1
Inverarity	54	C5
Inverbervie	55	G2
Inverebrie	51	E4
Inverkeilor	51	E5
Inverkeithny	50	B3
Invernettie	51	G3
Inverquharity	54	C4
Inverquhomery	51	F3
Inverugie	51	G3
Inverurie	53	E1
Invery House	53	D4
Inverythan	50	C3
Ironside	51	D2

J

Jackstown	50	C4
Johnshaven	55	F3
Johnston Mains	55	F3
Jordanstone	54	A5

K

Kebholes	50	B2
Keig	52	D2
Keilhill	50	C2
Keillor	54	A5
Keithock	55	E3
Kemnay	53	E2
Kennerty	53	D4
Kennethmont	52	C1

Kildrummy	52	B2
Kinblethmont	55	E5
Kincaldrum	54	C5
Kincardine O'Neil	52	C4
Kincorth	53	G3
Kincraig	53	G1
Kinellar	53	F2
Kingsford *Aberdeenshire*	50	C3
Kingsford *Aberdeenshire*	52	C2
Kingsford *Aberdeen*	53	F3
Kingsmuir	54	C5
Kingswells	53	F3
Kinharrachie	51	E4
Kinknockie	51	F3
Kinloch	54	A5
Kinmuck	53	F2
Kinnadie	51	E3
Kinneff	55	G2
Kinnell	55	E4
Kinnettles	54	C5
Kinnordy	54	B4
Kintocher	52	C3
Kintore	53	E2
Kiplaw Croft	51	F4
Kirkbuddo	54	D5
Kirkhill	55	E3
Kirkinch	54	B5
Kirkney	50	A4
Kirkstile	50	A4
Kirkton *Aberdeenshire*	52	D1
Kirkton *Aberdeenshire*	50	B2
Kirkton *Aberdeenshire*	52	D2
Kirkton *Angus*	54	C5
Kirkton of Airlie	54	B4
Kirkton of Bourtie	53	F1
Kirkton of Craig	55	F4
Kirkton of Culsalmond	50	B4
Kirkton of Durris	53	E4
Kirkton of Glenbuchat	52	A2
Kirkton of Glenisla	54	A3
Kirkton of Kingoldrum	54	B4
Kirkton of Logie Buchan	53	G1
Kirkton of Maryculter	53	F4
Kirkton of Menmuir	54	D3
Kirkton of Rayne	50	B4
Kirkton of Skene	53	F3
Kirktonhill	55	E3
Kirktown	51	F2
Kirktown of Alvah	50	B1
Kirktown of Auchterless	50	C3
Kirktown of Deskford	50	A1
Kirktown of Fetteresso	53	F5
Kirktown of Slains	51	F5
Kirriemuir	54	B4
Knabbygates	50	A2
Knaven	51	D3
Knock	50	A2
Knowes of Elrick	50	B2
Knowhead	51	E2

L

Ladysford	51	E1
Laithers	50	B3
Landerberry	53	E3
Largie	50	B4
Largue	50	B3
Lary	52	A3
Lauchintilly	53	E2
Laurencekirk	55	F2
Leask	51	F4
Leitfie	54	A5
Lemnas	50	D1
Leochel-Cushnie	52	C2
Leschangie	53	E2
Leslie	52	C1
Lessendrum	50	A3
Letham	54	D5
Lethenty	50	D3
Ley	52	C2
Leylodge	53	E2
Leys *Aberdeenshire*	51	F2
Leys *Aberdeenshire*	52	B3
Leys of Cossans	54	B5
Leysmill	55	E5
Limehillock	50	A2
Lindertis	54	B4
Linhead	50	B2
Linn of Muick Cottage	52	B4
Lintmill	50	A1
Little Brechin	55	D3
Little Dens	51	F3

Little Idoch	50	C3
Little Ley	52	D2
Loanhead	51	E4
Lochlair	54	D5
Lochside	55	F3
Logie *Angus*	55	E3
Logie *Angus*	54	B4
Logie Coldstone	52	B3
Logie Newton	50	B4
Logie Pert	55	E3
Longdrum	53	G2
Longhill	51	E2
Longlands	52	B1
Longmanhill	50	C1
Longside	51	F3
Lour	54	C5
Lownie Moor	54	C5
Lumphanan	52	C3
Lumsden	52	B1
Lunan	55	E4
Lunanhead	54	C4
Lunderton	51	G3
Luthermuir	55	E3
Lyne	53	E3
Lyne of Skene	53	E2

M

Macduff	50	C1
Macterry	50	C3
Mains of Balgavies	54	D4
Mains of Balhall	54	D3
Mains of Ballindarg	54	C4
Mains of Culsh	51	D3
Mains of Dillavaird	53	E5
Mains of Drum	53	F3
Mains of Dudwick	51	E4
Mains of Fedderate	51	D3
Mains of Glack	53	E1
Mains of Glassaugh	50	A1
Mains of Glenbuchat	52	A2
Mains of Linton	53	E3
Mains of Melgund	54	D4
Mains of Pitfour	51	E3
Mains of Pittrichie	53	F1
Mains of Thornton	55	E2
Mannofield	53	G3
Marcus	54	D4
Marnoch	50	A2
Maryhill	50	D3
Marykirk	55	E3
Maryton	55	E4
Marywell *Aberdeenshire*	53	G4
Marywell *Aberdeenshire*	52	C4
Marywell *Angus*	55	E5
Mastrick	53	F3
Maud	51	E3
Mayen	50	A3
Meigle	54	A5
Meikle Strath	55	E2
Meikle Tarty	53	G1
Meikle Wartle	50	C4
Melgum	52	B3
Melrose	50	C1
Memsie	51	E1
Memus	54	C4
Menie House	53	G1
Mergie	53	E5
Methlick	51	D4
Mid Ardlaw	51	E1
Mid Beltie	52	D3
Mid Cairncross	54	D2
Middle Drums	54	D4
Middlehill	50	D3
Middleton *Aberdeenshire*	53	F2
Middleton *Angus*	55	D5
Middleton of Potterton	53	G2
Middleton Park	53	G2
Midtown of Barras	53	F5
Migvie	52	B3
Milbethill	50	B2
Mill of Colp	50	C3
Mill of Elrick	51	E3
Mill of Kingoodie	53	F1
Mill of Monquich	53	F4
Mill of Uras	55	G2
Millbank	51	F3
Millbreck	51	F3
Millburn *Aberdeenshire*	52	C1
Millburn *Aberdeenshire*	50	B4
Millden	53	G2

Milldens 54 D4
Milltimber 53 F3
Milltown 52 B2
Milltown of Craigston 50 C2
Milltown of Rothiemay 50 A3
Milltown of Towie 52 B2
Milton *Angus* 54 B5
Milton *Moray* 50 A1
Milton of Auchinhove 52 C3
Milton of Campfield 52 D3
Milton of Coldwells 51 E4
Milton of Cullerlie 53 E3
Milton of Cushnie 52 C2
Milton of Inveramsay 53 E1
Milton of Noth 52 C1
Milton of Tullich 52 A4
Minnes 53 G1
Minnonie 50 C1
Mintlaw 51 F3
Monkshill 50 C3
Monteach 51 D3
Montgarrie 52 C2
Montrose 55 F4
Monymusk 53 D2
Morphie 55 F3
Moss-side 50 A2
Mossat 52 B2
Mosshead 50 A4
Mosside of Ballinshoe 54 C4
Mosston 54 D5
Mounie Castle 53 E1
Mountblairy 50 B2
Mowtie 53 F5
Muchalls 53 F4
Muckletown 52 C1
Muir of Fowlis 52 C2
Muirden 50 C2
Muirhead 52 C2
Muirtack 51 E4
  Aberdeenshire
Muirtack 50 D3
  Aberdeenshire
Muirton of Ballochy 55 E3
Muiryfold 50 C2
Mundurno 53 G2
Murthill 54 C4
Myrebird 53 E4

N
Nether Crimond 53 F1
Nether Glasslaw 51 D2
Nether Handwick 54 B5
Nether Kinmundy 51 F3
Nether Lenshie 50 B3
Nether Pitforthie 55 G2
Netherbrae 50 C2
Netherley 53 F4
Nethermuir 51 E3
Netherton 54 D4
New Aberdour 51 D1
New Alyth 54 A5
New Byth 50 D2
New Deer 51 D3
New Leeds 51 E2
New Leslie 52 C1
New Mains of Ury 53 F5
New Pitsligo 51 D2
Newbigging 53 F4
  Aberdeenshire
Newbigging *Angus* 54 A5
Newburgh 51 E2
  Aberdeenshire
Newburgh 53 G1
  Aberdeenshire
Newmachar 53 F2
Newmill *Aberdeenshire* 53 E5
Newmill *Aberdeenshire* 51 D3
Newmill *Aberdeenshire* 53 F1
Newmill of Inshewan 54 C3
Newnoth 50 A4
Newseat 50 C4
Newton 51 F3
Newtonhill 53 G4
Newtonmill 55 E3
Newtyle 54 A5
Nigg 53 G3
Noranside 54 C3
North Essie 51 F2
North Millbrex 50 D3
North Tarbothill 53 G2
Northburnhill 50 D3
Northfield 50 D1
  Aberdeenshire

O
Northfield *Aberdeen* 53 F3
Northmuir 54 B4

O
Oathlaw 54 C4
Ogil 54 C3
Old Aberdeen 53 G3
Old Craig 53 G1
Old Crombie 50 A2
Old Deer 51 E3
Old Kinnernie 53 E3
Old Leslie 52 C1
Old Rattray 51 F2
Old Rayne 53 D1
Oldhall 52 B4
Oldmeldrum 53 F1
Oldmill 52 C3
Oldtown of Ord 50 B2
Oldwhat 51 D2
Ordhead 53 D2
Ordie 52 B3
Orrok House 53 G2
Overbrae 50 D2
Overton *Aberdeenshire* 53 E2
Overton *Aberdeen* 53 F2
Oyne 53 D1

P
Padanaram 54 C4
Park 50 A2
Parkford 54 C4
Parkhill 55 E5
Parkneuk 55 F2
Pathhead 55 F3
Pearsie 54 B4
Peathill 51 E1
Pennan 50 D1
Percie 52 C4
Perkhill 52 C3
Pert 55 E3
Peterculter 53 F3
Peterhead 51 G3
Petty 50 C4
Pettymuick 53 G1
Phesdo 55 E2
Pitblae 51 E1
Pitcaple 53 E1
Pitfichie 53 D2
Pitinnan 50 C4
Pitkennedy 54 D4
Pitmedden 53 F1
Pitmuies 55 D5
Pitmunie 53 D2
Pittodrie House 53 D1
Plaidy 50 C2
Port Elphinstone 53 E2
Port Erroll 51 F4
Portlethen 53 G4
Portlethen Village 53 G4
Portsoy 50 A1
Potarch 52 D4
Potterton 53 G2
Protstonhill 50 D1

Q
Quilquox 51 E4

R
Raemoir House 53 D4
Rathen 51 F1
Raxton 51 D4
Redcastle 55 E4
Redcloak 53 F5
Redford *Aberdeenshire* 55 F3
Redford *Angus* 55 D5
Redheugh 54 C3
Redhill *Aberdeenshire* 50 B4
Redhill *Aberdeenshire* 53 E3
Redhill *Moray* 50 A3
Redhouse 52 C1
Rescobie 54 D4
Reswallie 54 D4
Rhynie 52 B1
Rickarton 53 F5
Rinmore 52 B2
Roadside of Kinneff 55 G2
Rora 51 F2
Rorandle 53 D2
Rosehearty 51 E1
Rosehill 52 C4
Rossie Farm School 55 E4
Rothiebrisbane 50 C4
Rothienorman 50 C4

Rottal 54 B3
Runtaleave 54 A3
Ruthrieston 53 G3
Ruthven *Aberdeenshire* 50 A3
Ruthven *Angus* 54 A5

S
Saint Combs 51 F1
Saint Cyrus 55 F3
Saint Fergus 51 G2
Saint Katherines 50 C4
Saint Vigeans 55 E5
Sandend 50 A1
Sandfordhill 51 G3
Sandhaven 51 E1
Sauchen 53 D2
Sauchieburn 55 E3
Scotston 55 F2
Seatown *Aberdeenshire* 51 G2
Seatown *Moray* 50 A1
Shanzie 54 A4
Shielhill 54 C4
Shiels 53 D3
Sillyearn 50 A2
Silvermoss 50 D4
Sinnahard 52 B2
Skares 50 B4
Skelmonae 51 D4
Skelmuir 51 E3
Slack 50 A4
Slains Park 55 G2
Slioch 50 A4
Smallburn 51 F3
South Blackbog 50 C4
South Flobbets 50 C4
South Kirkton 53 E3
South Redbriggs 50 C3
South Upper Barrack 51 E3
Southend 50 C3
Southmuir 54 B4
Spittal of Glenmuick 52 A5
Springleys 50 C4
Steinmanhill 50 C3
Stirling 51 G3
Stonehaven 53 F5
Stoneywood 53 F2
Stracathro 55 E3
Strachan 53 D4
Straloch 53 F1
Strathdon 52 A2
Strathgirnock 52 A4
Strichen 51 E2
Stuartfield 51 E3
Sunnyside 53 F4

T
Tanglandford 51 D4
Tannachie 53 E5
Tannadice 54 C4
Tarfside 52 B5
Tarland 52 B3
Tarves 51 D4
Tavelty 53 E2
Tayock 55 E4
Templewood 55 E3
Tepersie Castle 52 C1
Teuchan 51 F4
Tewel 53 F5
Thainston 55 E2
Thainstone House 53 E2
The Banking 50 C4
The Birks 53 E3
The Burn 55 D2
The Drums 54 B3
The Neuk 53 E4
Thomastown 50 A4
Thornton 54 B5
Thornyhill 55 E2
Thunderton 51 F3
Tifty 50 C3
Tigerton 54 D3
Tillery 53 G1
Tillyarblet 54 D3
Tillybirloch 53 D3
Tillycairn Castle 53 D2
Tillycorthie 53 G1
Tillydrine 52 D4
Tillyfar 51 D3
Tillyfour 53 C2
Tillyfourie 52 D2
Tillygreig 53 F1
Tillypronie 52 B3
Tipperty *Aberdeenshire* 53 E5

Tipperty *Aberdeenshire* 53 G1
Tocher 50 B4
Todlachie 53 D2
Toll of Birness 51 F4
Torbeg 52 A3
Tornaveen 52 D3
Torphins 52 D3
Torrancroy 52 A2
Torry 53 G3
Torterston 51 F3
Toux 51 E2
Towie *Aberdeenshire* 51 D1
Towie *Aberdeenshire* 52 C1
Towie *Aberdeenshire* 52 B2
Trinity 55 E3
Tulloch 53 D4
Tullochvenus 52 C3
Tulloes 54 D5
Tullyfergus 54 A5
Tullynessle 52 C2
Turclossie 51 D2
Turin 54 D4
Turriff 50 C2

U
Udny Green 53 F1
Udny Station 53 G1
Union Croft 53 F4
Upper Boyndlie 51 E1
Upper Burnhaugh 53 F4
Upper Hawkhillock 51 F4
Upper Lochton 53 D4
Upper Muirskie 53 F4
Upper Ridinghill 51 F2

W
Wardhouse 50 A4
Wartle 52 C3
Waterhill of Bruxie 51 E3
Waterloo 51 F4
Waterside 52 A2
  Aberdeenshire
Waterside 51 F5
  Aberdeenshire
Weachyburn 50 B2
Wedderlairs 51 D4
West Cairncake 50 D3
West Muir 55 D3
West Park 53 E4
Wester Badentyre 50 C2
Wester Culbeuchly 50 B1
Wester Fintray 53 F2
Wester Foffarty 54 C5
Wester Greenskares 50 C1
Wester Ord 53 F3
Westerton 53 E4
  Aberdeenshire
Westerton *Angus* 55 E4
Westhall 53 D1
Westhill 53 F3
Westmuir 54 B4
Westside 54 F4
Wheedlemont 52 B1
Wheen 54 B2
Whigstreet 54 C5
Whinnyfold 51 F4
Whitebog 51 E2
Whitecairns 53 G2
Whitefield 53 E1
Whiteford 53 E1
Whitehills 50 B1
Whitehouse 52 D2
Whiterashes 53 F1
Whitestone 52 D4
Whitestripe 51 E2
Whitewell 51 E1
Whitlam 53 F1
Witton 55 D3
Woodend 53 D2
Woodhead 50 C4
Woodside 53 G3
Wrae 50 C2
Wrangham 50 B4

Y
Yonder Bognie 50 A3
Ythanwells 50 B4
Ythsie 51 D4